THE JAMAICAN BOBSLED CAPTAIN

Dudley "Tal" Stokes and the untold story of struggle,
suffering and redemption behind Cool Runnings

BEN STUBENBERG

Nonfiction
Sports / Biography

Books from Inside the Reef

Cover photo courtesy Leo Campbell. Permission to use deeply appreciated.

Back cover photo courtesy Denise Stokes. Permission to use deeply appreciated.

ISBN 979-8-35096-816-3

eBook ISBN 979-8-35096-817-0

"Let me not then die ingloriously without a struggle, but let me first do some great things that shall be told among men hereafter." —Homer

"Life is a struggle. Anything worth doing in life is a struggle. And anytime you struggle, you are going to suffer. People think suffering is something to be avoided. No! Suffering is reality." —Tal Stokes

DEDICATION

This book is dedicated to the first Jamaican bobsledders and all those who supported them on their improbable odyssey.

PRAISE FOR *THE JAMAICAN BOBSLED CAPTAIN*

Ben Stubenberg's *The Jamaican Bobsled Captain* is a compelling and unputdownable truth telling story about wide-eyed dreamers and doers and their achievements. His truth telling reminds us that, in the end, we are all very grateful they never gave up. Thank you Ben!

David Mason
Author, *Marching with the Devil* and
Walk Across Australia: the First Solo Crossing.

In *The Jamaican Bobsled Captain* Ben Stubenberg weaves together astounding hidden details to reveal the "real" story of Tal Stokes and the unlikely Jamaican bobsled team. Not only will readers be encouraged by Tal's tale of determination and providence but be enlightened by a portrayal of life in the Caribbean and the greater world of competitive sports. Be prepared for lots of "hobbin' and bobbin'" as the book hurtles through its own twists and turns.

Kathy Borsuk
Editor, *Times of the Islands* magazine

The Jamaican Bobsled Captain delves into the politics and the emotional and financial cost of developing a world class sports team from scratch with deeply respectful portraits of people and events. Based upon extensive interviews with the participants and solid research on the sport, Stubenberg's book aptly conveys the courage and persistence required to compete. It is a riveting and delightful book!

Andrea Stringos
Founder, The Book Club That Swims

TABLE OF CONTENTS

PROLOGUE

first saw Dudley "Tal" Stokes at an island fish fry when a friend discretely pointed to him and said in a low voice,

"You know who that guy is? He's the captain of the first Jamaican bobsled team, the one the movie *Cool Runnings* was based on."

I turned slowly, trying not to look too obvious, and glanced at the tall, fit, husky man with the close-cropped graying hair. He seemed oblivious to the festivities all around and focused intently on the guy he was talking to, as if he were the only person at the event. I nodded to my friend to acknowledge the sighting of a man that everyone knows about, but hardly anyone would recognize his face or name. And there he was, a global celebrity, just 20 feet away.

One might think that living on a small island like Providenciales (commonly called "Provo") in the Turks and Caicos Islands, everyone would know everyone and run into each other all the time. But it doesn't work that way. You can go months, sometimes years, without seeing someone you met, or even a friend, if you don't make an effort to keep in touch. So, I didn't run into Tal for another four years when he showed up at Rickie's, a popular beach bar where I sometimes drop in. He did not scan the place to see who he might know and didn't seem to care who else was there except the person he was talking to with a noticeable intensity. No smiles, no waves of the hand, and no need to be greeted, flattered, or show interest in getting to know other people. He seemed somewhat unapproachable and maybe an introvert, but certainly someone supremely secure in his skin.

Two more years pass, and I see Tal on the beach at sunset with his family and a couple of friends. I had had a recent business dealing with his wife, Denise, and she introduced me. Tal shook my hand, looked at me without so much as an expressive wrinkle on his face, and said nothing as he assessed me. But it was the start of an acquaintance that eventually led to a beer and later allowed me to slide in the question:

"Can I tell your story in the next edition of the local magazine, *Times of the Islands*?"

Tal shrugged, which signaled a kind of yes. But Tal doesn't do anything half-heartedly. When he commits to something, however nonchalant, he's all in.

I entitled the article "TCI Bobsledder" because, unbeknownst to all but a tiny handful of people, Tal was actually born on Grand Turk, not Jamaica. So, with a bit of hubris, I angled the story to claim him also as our own Turks and Caicos bobsledder (my apologies to Jamaica). As it turned out, there were quite a few surprising untold tales in the course of my interviews with him. Tal did not hold back expounding on the riveting details of the team's journey from a dreamed-up fantasy by a couple of Americans to violently crashing on track at the 1988 Winter Olympics in Calgary to eventually entering bobsledding's elite.

What struck me the most was Tal's tenacity and force-of-personality to hold the team together when the prospect of failure constantly loomed and bad luck struck over and over. It would have been easy for him to walk away from the whole crazy notion of Caribbean islanders even engaging in a sport like bobsledding and then audaciously aspiring to compete on a world-class level when so many thought the Jamaicans were a joke. As I came to understand, Tal's life story growing up in Jamaica with stern parents and as a military officer who became a helicopter pilot laid the foundation for the kind of grit and fortitude that it takes to go up against the best. The movie *Cool Runnings* missed the far more compelling story of

Tal and the Jamaican bobsled team's struggle, suffering and redemption, along with a cast of adventurous, risk-taking, and eccentric characters who helped them along the way. I knew a book was waiting to be written.

But I had never written a book. Only a slew of articles, scores of speeches, and a few coldly analytical pieces on foreign threats. (Not counting memos up the chain of command.) And here I was asking Tal if I could tell his story, his biography as captain of one of the most iconic sports teams of the second half of the 20th century, the team which inspired a hugely successful Disney movie (mostly fiction) that had the world cheering. Tal graciously put his confidence in me, for which I am forever grateful. He gave me a couple of dozen more hours of interviews and put me in touch with most of the players still alive. All of them generously shared with me their role and perspectives in the epic Jamaican bobsled quest, and didn't hold back either. So here it is. Tuck yourselves in, hold on tight, and enjoy the ride!

PART ONE:

ISLAND ROOTS

CHAPTER 1

THE START

On a warm and windy February morning in 1988, the captain of the first Jamaican bobsled team stood at the top of the Olympic track in Calgary and tried hard to stifle the taunting demons swirling around him. He stared down the steep chute coated with fresh, fast ice that glared back in the bright sun. In the stands, excited fans from winter sports countries waved billowing banners and rattled cowbells that filled the air with loud and boisterous joy. But this time, the flags fluttered and the bells rang for the improbable sight of four Black men from a tropical Caribbean island as they moved their sled to the start blocks.

On any other day, the encouraging goodwill from bobsled fans might have buoyed the spirits of the driver of the four-man bobsled team, Dudley "Tal" Stokes. But not today. Tal had woken up early with the Olympic flu and a temperature of 103°F. Unwilling to risk being tested positive for a banned substance, he took no medication. Shaking off the grogginess, he headed to the bobsled track to inspect conditions before the start of the final two heats less than an hour away. As he walked the winding chute—a standard protocol before the race—he closed his eyes and visualized each curve he would steer through at breakneck speed. He imagined what the turns would feel like as 5Gs of gravity force pressed his spine into the bottom of the sled. Then he bent down to glide the palm of his hand over the glaze of ice on the track to feel the cold and firmness. In a lapse, probably from the flu, Tal slipped and fell and smacked his right collarbone hard.

5

Suppressing the searing pain shooting down his shoulder, Tal met with his teammates—Devon Harris, Michael White, and Chris Stokes (Tal's brother)—and prepped the sled for final inspection by officials. As the team's only driver, Tal was not about to drop out and end Jamaica's Winter Olympics debut. Not after all they had gone through to get there. Not with 40 million pairs of eyes watching on TVs around the world. The fever and agony could have been easy outs, but the pressure Tal put on himself to compete overrode all of that.

It did not matter that he had fewer than ten practice runs in the four-man sled. Nor did it matter that the team had acquired status as media darlings just for showing up, even though they had not accomplished anything of significance. Indeed, after two poor runs during the previous day's heats, Jamaica had only managed to place second from the bottom.

If the team could push the sled a little faster today. If Tal could just steer the sled down the line a little straighter and bump the walls less. If a little luck came their way, they might shave off a few more hundredths of a second, enough to climb in the standings and earn them a respectable finish. Respect mattered, if nothing else than to validate that they were there to compete, not be a sideshow. That and the pure rush of dopamine pumping through the brain while sliding down a narrow chute of ice at more than 80 miles an hour—the unmatched high of cheating death one more time, which brings bobsledders back again and again.

As first-aiders iced Tal's battered shoulder and numbed the pain with spray, he looked around for the man who had taught him and the team how to push and drive the sled and who had continued to mentor them. Tal liked his reassuring presence, but he was nowhere to be found. Minutes before the start, one of the team organizers pulled Tal aside and said,

"He's gone."

"What do you mean 'gone'?" Tal asked.

"He flew out this morning, back to New York."

"Why?"

"I don't know. He just called me to say he was going."

Shaken, Tal looked up at the blue sky to put himself into a deep state of relaxation as he mentally rehearsed the flow of the sled from start to finish. He shut out the worsening flu, the aching collarbone, and the frenzy around him. He shed his doubts about his skill as a newcomer to the sport and the coach's jolting absence. Mustering all the strength he could to focus on the present, Tal pulled down his goggles—the physical signal to execute—and slowly wrapped his fingers around the push bar. On the count of three, the four men sprinted as one, pushing over 600 lbs of metal and fiberglass faster and faster. One by one, they leaped into the sled, nimble as ballerinas, before tucking tightly together and hurling themselves down the ice that would inspire millions and change their lives forever.

CHAPTER 2

POPULAR NARRATIVES

The first popular narrative of how the Jamaican bobsled team originated goes something like this: Two American friends are sitting in a bar in Kingston, knocking back rum and Cokes one after the other. In an alcoholic haze, they look up on the TV screen and see the Jamaican Push Cart Derby championships. To them, the carts charging down a hill and sometimes crashing look remarkably like bobsleds plunging down ice tracks and sometimes crashing. And that's when the preposterous idea of creating a bobsled team—a Jamaican bobsled team—hits them.

Why not? Jamaica has great sprinters and guys who can steer push carts. The two Americans scribble down what needs to be done on a napkin, then go out and pitch the concept and recruit a team. In Cinderella fashion, the Jamaicans make it to the 1988 Winter Olympics in Calgary, where they become instant celebrities with adoring fans. Hollywood comes knocking and wants to make a movie about them.

The second and more well-known narrative is the 1993 hit movie *Cool Runnings*. In this version, a top Jamaican sprinter trips during the Summer Olympic track trials and doesn't make the team. Frustrated but determined, he learns about bobsledding and decides to pursue a new Olympic dream. He recruits two other sprinters and a pushcart racer, and together they approach a disgraced American bobsled coach who happens to hang out in a Kingston bar. Even though the gold medal-winning coach had been kicked out of the bobsledding world for cheating in a race years earlier, he is the only one around who can help them.

The slovenly drunk coach in *Cool Runnings*, played by the late great John Candy, refuses at first. But the Jamaicans manage to persuade him to train them as bobsledders from scratch for the 1988 Winter Olympics. The would-be bobsledders practice in pushcarts, comically flailing at every turn, before making it to the big time in Calgary to the surprise of everyone. They get lots of attention, as well as some insults, before crashing the sled and proudly carrying it across the finish line to wild cheers.

Neither one of these narratives comes close to the real story, which unfolded quite differently with far more human drama. That is the tale that needs to be told. Two Americans at a bar did kindle the idea of forming a Jamaican bobsled team. Some very good athletes did compete as bobsledders at the Winter Olympics. They did become a popular phenomenon, and the sled did crash in Calgary. Other than that, the tidy yarns spun into popular culture, including the movie, are largely fiction.

While *Cool Runnings* captured popular imagination with its light-hearted, comedic angle, it missed the audacious gambles and unforeseen serendipity that played out behind the scenes. It didn't show how characters, colorful and eccentric, serious and steely-minded, and from vastly different backgrounds, fought and united to race down a sheet of ice again and again. And the movie revealed nothing of the pain, struggle, and soul-testing sacrifice that ultimately turned the Jamaican bobsledders into fierce competitors. They started as an aberration that should not have happened but redeemed themselves as contenders who beat most of the best in the world.

One can argue that we should not hold the movie to such lofty standards and just enjoy it for what it is—playful, popular Hollywood entertainment that, in fact, wildly succeeded. The movie ended up grossing $154 million worldwide, the highest for any sports comedy. So due credit goes to the Hollywood producer and director for connecting with a broad, global appeal.

Unfortunately, because of the movie, most people have come to see Jamaican bobsledders as lovable jesters, which overshadows their hard-fought accomplishments. The incongruity of Black men from the Caribbean entering a "white" sport of snow and ice resonates for comic relief, but it also takes away from a team that mastered and ultimately shined in a demanding and dangerous sport. It's fair to ask: would a comedy be made about other sports legends who also had to deal with mocking doubters to break through barriers?

There is a richer story to chronicle here—a theme that has resonated through the ages about wide-eyed dreamers and determined doers set on a mission to achieve the seemingly impossible. One might believe that higher powers foreordain the convergence of forces or that it is all a matter of random chance. Either way, a serendipitous confluence of people and opportunities opens a door for the bold to do something that's never been done. Such universal journeys imbue us with a sense of possibilities while exposing the sheer unpredictability of life. How we handle the obstacles strewn before us along the way tests our resolve to prevail and ultimately determines our character. That is, after all, the saga of our species that, on occasion, plays out through the transcendent power of sport.

The story of how Tal Stokes came to lead the iconic Jamaican bobsled team adheres to this theme of leaping into the unknown for the adventure of finding what's there and if they have the right stuff. Wrested from the security and orderliness of an assured army career as a well-regarded helicopter pilot, he is thrust onto the world stage to pursue an implausible Olympic quest for which neither he nor his teammates has any point of reference. In pursuing that quest, they too faced a question as old as the one posed in Homer's *The Iliad*: Is it better to live a long and peaceful life of obscurity or risk a short life that results in great fame? The Jamaicans answered by going for broke and taking a shot at glory.

CHAPTER 3

ISLAND BORN

Tal's unlikely odyssey began before he was born when a tramp steamer called the *Carib Queen* chugged in from Jamaica and anchored off the shore of the small, hot, flat, dry island of Grand Turk in the Turks and Caicos. A newly married couple, Pastor Dudley Stokes and Blossom O'Meally-Nelson Stokes, carefully stepped into a rowboat rocking in the choppy sea. Blossom, who turned 21 that day, cradled the pet Siamese cat she had brought and wondered what exactly she had gotten herself into. A dozen or so Baptist parishioners, dressed in their Sunday best, warmly welcomed the couple when the boat pulled onto the sandy shore. The parishioners had been without a pastor for some time and eagerly awaited the new minister from the Jamaican Baptist Union. Ordained one month earlier and just 23 years old, Pastor Dudley accepted the "call" straight out of theology school and volunteered for the mission. The year was 1961.

The mesmerizing hues of blue and turquoise water and miles of idyllic white beaches could not hide or relieve the poverty and despair of their new home. The Mission House, where the couple would live, had no running water and no electricity. Very little food grew in the rocky limestone soil, so the people depended on sloops arriving from Haiti every six weeks loaded up with fruits and vegetables. At least the local fishermen brought in fish, conch, and lobster to feed the island when other food ran low.

For Blossom, the move from Jamaica to Grand Turk, leaving behind her family and all that she knew, would soon turn into a five-year ordeal that almost destroyed her. She had been born into an upper-middle-class family in Kingston that encouraged exploration and creative expression. Her parents enrolled her in a fine boarding school for girls, where she excelled, even if defiant from time to time. At age 20, she won a scholarship to attend a university in Toronto that would ensure she would follow in the footsteps of her well-educated parents. Graduation from a fine college would also make it more likely for Blossom to find a spouse who matched her social status and continue a comfortable upper-middle-class lifestyle.

Instead, she fell in love with a good-looking, charming, ambitious, and supremely confident theology student from a poor, working-class home in a Kingston ghetto. Growing up, Pastor Dudley had seen far too many young men like him succumb to the lure of gangs and end up in prison. He too had his scrapes with the law before being sent to reform school. Deciding to take his life in a different direction, he became a Baptist preacher with a rigid faith that forbade dancing or watching movies. The religious requirements could not have contrasted more sharply with Blossom's liberal and open-minded Anglican persuasion. Baptist women could not even wear pants or even acknowledge their own sexuality, as Blossom would later lament. In Jamaica, as in all of the West Indies, religious affiliation often mirrored and exacerbated class divisions.

For some in Blossom's family, Pastor Dudley's dark skin did not sit well when compared to Blossom's lighter brown complexion, which reflected a blend of Irish, Anglo, and African ancestry. Indeed, Blossom's family could trace their family history back to the 16th-century Irish pirate Queen Grace O'Mally, as well as the British Royal Navy's greatest hero, Admiral Horatio Nelson. The whole engagement to Pastor Dudley appeared, at best, unsuitable and bordered on scandal. But her father and mother decided to make the best of it and held out the possibility of bringing Pastor Dudley into their class.

Most distressing for Blossom was the expectation by her new husband and the Baptist Church that she would take on a subservient role as the wife of a minister. As a young lady who hardly ever had to cook or clean because these chores were tended to by cooks and domestic servants, Blossom had some big adjustments ahead of her. Nonetheless, she made a decision to go all-in to make it work, including being re-baptized as a Baptist.

As the itinerant preacher-missionary, it fell to Pastor Stokes to visit each inhabited island of the Turks and Caicos in a small sloop or sometimes a boat powered by a single sputtering outboard engine. These trips were often fraught with peril, especially when crossing the 24-mile open ocean passage between Grand Turk and South Caicos. Sudden squalls could quickly swamp and sink a vessel. Or the engine could simply conk out and set a boat adrift with little hope of rescue. Dozens, if not hundreds, of Islanders had lost their lives during voyages like this, which sharpened the presence of death. Despite the hazards, Pastor Stokes never wavered in his commitment to reach out to everyone. When he arrived at the sparsely populated outer islands, parishioners eagerly greeted him, usually bringing a donkey for him to ride so he didn't have to walk to the village.

Both Pastor Dudley and Blossom had big hearts. Nothing reflected their kindness more than when they took into their household a teen-age boy, Sandy Lightbourne. At 14, Sandy had moved to Grand Turk from the island of Middle Caicos to attend the only high school in Turks & Caicos. Almost all of the other high school teens from other islands had some family on Grand Turk whom they could live with. But Sandy didn't, and for almost three years, he stayed with a series of itinerate bachelor Baptist preachers who came from Jamaica for six months at a time.

When Pastor Dudley and Blossom met Sandy, they all bonded right away. Knowing Sandy's unstable situation and loneliness, Pastor Dudley and Blossom essentially "adopted" Sandy into their family, even though he wasn't much younger than them. That profoundly heartfelt decision would give their own soon-to-be-born children an older brother to look up to. Just as important, Pastor Dudley and Blossom's choice would deeply influence

Sandy and all the children to be mindful of life's defining moments and embrace them.

Not quite able to shed her upbringing, Blossom took it upon herself to form the first Baptist Women's Federation in the islands. The new association gave local Baptist women a small slice of independence and empowerment through their charity work. At times, Blossom found herself, along with Pastor Dudley, invited to socialize with what passed for the upper class of Grand Turk, mainly government ministers, leaders of the business community, and a few American and British ex-patriots, or "expats." On these occasions, she felt in her element again for a few brief hours before returning to the tedious role of dutiful wife in the shadow of her husband.

At the time, the Turks and Caicos Islands and Jamaica were colonies of Great Britain, with Turks and Caicos being the far less developed of the two. In fact, the Turks and Caicos was so economically depressed that thousands of islanders migrated out to the nearby Bahamas to find work during the 1950s and 60s. In Grand Turk, at least, a small US Air Force missile tracking station created some jobs for locals and brought in a little revenue.

Five months after Pastor Dudley and Blossom had stepped ashore, American astronaut John Glenn's *Mercury* capsule splashed down less than 100 miles east of Grand Turk on February 20, 1962. A US Navy ship picked Glenn up and a helicopter flew him to Grand Turk. Just about everyone on the island turned out to greet the heralded astronaut outside the perimeter of the base, including Pastor Stokes and Blossom, now five months pregnant. No one wanted to miss out on this historic moment that put the Turks and Caicos on the map and on the front pages of newspapers around the world. Unfortunately, Glenn did not step out to greet the crowd, but Blossom somehow obtained a photograph of him in his space suit. After Vice President Lyndon Johnson flew into Grand Turk to take Glenn back to the US and a hero's welcome, the Turks and Caicos faded back into impoverished obscurity.

On June 22, 1962, Blossom gave birth to Dudley Talmage Stokes. The experience exposed Blossom to the paucity of medical services on the islands during the early 1960s. Without a hospital or even a regular doctor, any minor emergency could quickly turn into a life-threatening risk. Pregnant women who developed complications before and during childbirth were especially vulnerable. For too many, death came early and often. US medics from the tracking base would step in and do what they could, but they were not always on the island.

Once, a young Baptist theology student from Jamaica came to visit the Turks and Caicos for the summer. While in the tiny settlement of Conch Bar on the island of Middle Caicos, the man came down with acute appendicitis. Locals put him in a boat and sailed across the passage to Grand Turk for treatment. Sailing against the prevailing wind took all day, and by the time he arrived, his appendix had ruptured. Blossom helped to bring the suffering man to the clinic, but it was too late; she held his hand as he died screaming in agony. A mortician flew over from Jamaica in a four-seater single-engine plane the next day. He embalmed the young theology student as Pastor Dudley held the lantern and then put him in a body bag to take him back home. Blossom saw it all, and nightmares followed her for weeks.

When she became pregnant with Tal's younger brother, Chris, she took no chances and went back to Jamaica to have the baby. It turned out to be the right decision. Just five weeks after birth, Chris suffered from pyloric stenosis, a condition causing projectile vomiting and dehydration that put him on death's doorstep. He actually weighed less after five weeks than when he was born. By chance, a surgeon from India had just arrived in Jamaica. He recognized the symptoms and performed his first surgery on the island to save Chris.

Tal relished his early childhood on Grand Turk and the family-friendly culture of Turks and Caicos Islanders, with doors open to anyone. He freely explored the beaches and salt pond salinas amidst the flocks of flamingos and wild donkeys, barefoot and blissfully content with the little they had. But as happy as life was for him, Blossom was never able to bridge the gap between her former life in Jamaica and the burden of being an itinerant Baptist preacher's wife on a tiny island far from home. Despite the strains between Blossom and Pastor Dudley, or perhaps because of them, along with stern discipline, their children developed street smarts and an unshakable, headstrong confidence to fight back.

CHAPTER 4

GROWING STRONG

n 1966, the family moved back to Jamaica, where Pastor Dudley worked as a circuit preacher in the tiny village of Galina in St. Mary Parish on the island's rugged north coast. Blossom resumed her plans for higher education and enrolled in a local college, taking education courses. A couple of years later, she gave birth to a baby girl, Terry, who would grow up to give her brothers teasing grief as well as unwavering family support when they needed it most.

In this beautiful, but poor, section of Jamaica, deep green forests dotted by small farms slope down to tan sand beaches that spill out to a brilliant blue sea. Here, Ian Fleming built his house, Goldeneye, in Oracabessa Bay, and wrote his James Bond novels. He might not have completed any of these books if he had succumbed to the stunning views.

Fleming said, "I sat down at the red bullet-wood desk where I am now typing this and, for better or worse, wrote the first 12 best-selling thrillers that have sold around 20 million copies and have been translated into 23 languages. I wrote every one of them at this desk with the jalousies (shutters) closed around me so that I would not be distracted by the birds and the flowers and the sunshine outside until I had completed my daily stint."

In 1962, Jamaica had secured its independence from Great Britain. As the first British colony in the Caribbean to strike out on its own, Jamaica inspired others in the region to believe that they too could take on the responsibilities of self-governance and full nationhood. A robust nationalism swept the Caribbean islands with the aim of framing a common destiny, succeeding or failing on their own terms without colonial overseers. After more than three centuries, British influence remained strong in all aspects of life—language, law, education, and democratic governance. But the country's rich and raw past forged an identity that set Jamaican people apart.

* * *

Around 600 AD, Taino Indians canoed and sailed from Cuba and Hispañola to Jamaica and set up thriving communities. They called their new home *Xaymaca*, meaning "land of wood and water," which evolved into today's name, Jamaica. Arawak Indians followed a few hundred years later and settled alongside the Taino's. Christopher Columbus landed on the island's north coast at St. Ann's Bay during his second voyage to the Caribbean in 1494 and shipwrecked in the same place on his final voyage in 1503–1504. He barely survived the year before being rescued. During the course of the exploration and early settlement in the late 1400s and early 1500s, the Spanish nearly wiped out the indigenous peoples within the span of a generation through enslavement, murder, and disease. Some of the Indians managed to escape deep into the mountain valleys of Jamaica, where they built hidden camps.

The British drove out the Spanish in 1655 during a decisive battle in St. Mary's Parish and established their own settlements in Jamaica, including the infamous pirate base of Port Royal. Located at the mouth of present-day Kingston Harbour, Port Royal emerged as the largest, richest, and most notorious town in the Caribbean. Here, swashbuckling pirates of all stripes, most prominently Henry Morgan, found a safe haven to squander their plundered wealth, particularly from Spanish treasure ships they had raided with the tacit support of the British. This buccaneer paradise with its plethora of taverns and brothels soon gained a reputation as the "wickedest city on earth."

For all their plundering, however, the pirates were in some ways ahead of their time by instituting democratic elections for captains and equal sharing of the loot from raids. Moreover, as many as a quarter of the crew on pirate ships were escaped slaves who instantly transitioned from the oppression of bondage to equal status once onboard. In 1692, a massive earthquake, followed by a tsunami, destroyed the structures built on soft sand and submerged a good portion of the town. Survivors set up another community nearby on more solid ground that, in time, became the thriving city of Kingston.

Piracy continued through the first two decades of the 1700s until the British had no more use for pirates and managed to stamp most of them out. The conviction and hanging of the dashing pirate, "Calico Jack" Rackham, in 1720 in Kingston signaled the demise of piracy in the Caribbean. Officials placed his body in a cage to rot while suspended from a pole at the entrance to Kingston Harbour as a warning of the consequences for would-be pirates passing through. The court also convicted Rackham's cohorts, the legendary female pirates Anne Bonny and Mary Read, and sentenced them to hang as well. They were spared the gallows when they claimed to be "quick with child." A doctor confirmed they were indeed pregnant—a good six months along. Mary died in prison, probably during childbirth. Anne apparently managed to escape prison and Jamaica, possibly eased by a bribe from her well-to-do father in South Carolina, and disappeared.

By then, the lucrative sugar plantations had begun to dominate the island economy, all made possible by the labor of enslaved Africans cutting and processing cane under brutal conditions. Typically, an enslaved man would be worked to death within seven years of his arrival on the plantation. The average enslaved person's lifespan was 21 or 22 years. As with the Taino and Arawak people, the enslaved Africans would also escape into the remote mountains, where they established clandestine communities and sometimes integrated with the Indians.

Known as "Maroons," the escapees quickly became a thorn in the side of British authority. Using guerrilla tactics, they raided plantations, killed white overseers and militiamen, and freed slaves, often family members and friends, who joined them back in the hidden valleys. Sometimes Maroons took on the British Army itself with attacks on barracks. The skirmishes went on for 12 years, from 1728 to 1740, when the British, unable to subdue the fierce resistance, signed a treaty giving Maroons rights and land.

Another major slave rebellion called "Tacky's War" broke out in 1760 when an enslaved African chief from Ghana named Takyi organized a force to kill their enslavers. He also successfully attacked British fortifications but was soon overwhelmed by superior British forces that included, ironically, an alliance of Maroons that reflected the complicated history of Jamaica. Still, most Maroons held out and remained free deep in the mountains. The notion of fighting for freedom against the odds—and holding out—settled deeply into the Jamaican psyche and, today, forms an essential part of the national character.

*   *   *

Once while hanging out at the beach, quite possibly where Columbus once walked, Tal, then nine, challenged his brother Chris, who was younger by 18 months, to a race. Tal ran as fast as he could, but Chris beat him, twice, making painfully clear who was the better athlete at that young age. The embarrassing loss caused Tal to focus on soccer, where he earned the nickname "El Toro" for his bull-like tenacity. As a fullback, he often got out-dribbled by the forwards of the opposing team but always pursued them until he got the ball back. Chris would go on to become the Jamaican high school 100-meter sprint champion.

A few years later, the highly regarded all-boys Calabar High School in Kingston hired Pastor Dudley as the school's chaplain and Dean of Discipline. Baptist abolitionists established the school in the 1840s as a theological seminary to train black preachers. In the early 20th century, it evolved into a school to give boys from black working-class families an education on par with the education afforded to wealthy white boys in Jamaica. Over the years, the school could take credit for producing many of Jamaica's leaders in virtually every field, from politics to science to sports.

The school gave the Stokes family living quarters on the school campus and free tuition for both Tal and Chris. Pastor Dudley taught classes too and didn't spare the rod when he felt discipline was necessary. Once, when none of the students in class would reveal the name of a boy who had pulled a prank, Pastor Dudley gave a paddling to everyone. Notwithstanding his way-over-the-top punishment by today's standards, the boys respected him. Some would later recall that without Pastor Dudley's discipline, they would have gone down the path to joining gangs.

Blossom and Pastor Dudley sternly disciplined their own children and pushed them to study hard and work hard. Tal internalized his feelings while accepting the punishments with less resistance. Chris talked and sometimes fought back. Terry, the youngest, had no interest in studying and got away with everything. How they handled the family tensions would shape their passage into adulthood. Tal, the more introverted, found his gift for mastering complex details with precision. Chris, the extrovert, would excel at cultivating relationships. Terry, notwithstanding her resistance to school, stuck with it, did well, and attained high success as an educator like her parents.

Calabar also included, as part of its elective curriculum, a fine cadet corps called the Jamaican Combined Force. It was similar to the Junior Reserve Officer Training Corps in the US. When Pastor Dudley arrived, a very capable senior Calabar student, Leo Campbell, led the 120-strong company of cadets with the rank of sergeant major. When the teacher who oversaw the cadet corps as the "Officer in Command" departed, Pastor Dudley was tapped for the job. But he knew little about military culture or protocol, as his only exposure had been through a brief stint in a lower-standard cadet corps in reform school. So the awkward duty of teaching the school's Dean of Discipline, and now the new Officer in Command, fell to Leo. Pastor Dudley relied entirely on Leo to get it right, which meant how to properly put on the parade uniform, salute, and stand correctly. Pastor Dudley sometimes invited Leo to the family residence for private training.

On these visits, Leo met the Stokes brothers, Tal, who was two years younger, and Chris, who was three years younger. The age and grade differences between Leo and the Stokes brothers didn't allow them to develop much of a friendship at the time. Leo's esteemed position at the school as student leader of the corps, as well as "Head Boy," similar to student body president in a US high school, made him the cool, popular kid everyone looked up to. If that was not enough, Leo had also been named the manager of the school's formidable soccer team, where he saw Tal playing for the junior varsity "Colts" team. The paths of Leo and the Stokes brothers would cross again.

At age 15, Tal tried out for the varsity soccer squad but didn't make the cut. Deeply distressed and embarrassed again for his athletic failure, he went home and told his mother. Rather than just comfort Tal or urge him to try something else, Blossom immediately marched over to coach Atlee McKoy's office. She did not attempt to persuade the coach to reconsider his decision. Rather, she demanded to know why. The highly respected coach, a former English Premier League player and member of the Jamaican National Football Team, proceeded to tell her point by point why Tal wasn't good enough for the top-caliber team. Indeed, Calabar regularly won Jamaica's high school champion "Manning Cup" and was a clear favorite to win again that year.

Blossom took careful notes. When she returned home, she handed Tal a list of 16 weaknesses, saying, "These are the reasons you are not on the varsity team."

Upsetting as it was, the incident became a life lesson for Tal that he would never forget—break down your flaws and work on them.

Around that same time, Tal had found a record store in Kingston where he could buy the latest "45" vinyl record releases by reggae stars, especially his idol, Bob Marley. Once, as Tal was exiting the store, a huge man with dreadlocks and sunglasses sat on the steps that blocked his way to the sidewalk. Tal stopped and stared, not quite sure what to do. The big man, seemingly oblivious to his surroundings, launched into a passionate soliloquy to no one in particular about his struggles, abilities, opportunities, failures, and betrayals. He ended by saying, "When I release my 'Buckingham Palace,' the world will know. I am better than Bob Marley!"

The man on the steps turned out to be Peter Tosh, an original Wailer with Bob Marley who would go on to establish his own lasting legacy as one of Jamaica's greatest reggae singer-songwriters. His hits would include the album *Mystic Man* (1979), which featured the riveting crossover beat song "Buk-In-Hamm Palace." Tosh was shot dead in his Kingston home in 1987 during a vicious robbery, just as Tal was beginning his bobsled journey. But the self-taught musician's outrageous claims of going big while sitting alone on a stoop with nothing except enormous self-confidence—and then making it happen—stuck with Tal.

CHAPTER 5

AN OFFICER AND A PILOT

Afer graduating from Calabar High School and Cornwall College in Montego Bay in 1980, Tal passed the British "A" level exams and immediately enlisted in the Jamaican Defense Force (JDF) officer cadet program. He had never expressed the slightest interest in the military, so it came as quite a surprise to everyone. Tal embraced the discipline and challenges of military life and saw the career potential. The following year, JDF selected him to attend Great Britain's elite Royal Military Academy Sandhurst, which Leo had also attended two years earlier. (Tal actually wanted to attend the UK's Royal Marine Commando Training Centre, but, unbeknownst to Tal at the time, his father pulled strings to get him into the more prestigious Sandhurst.)

Tal continued to thrive in the strict and demanding Sandhurst environment. He took each course seriously and loved the opportunities to succeed. His ability to focus and break down problems that had started at Calabar became even more intense at Sandhurst. Whatever he did, he did to the extreme—totally engaged. In the Signals course, Tal got perfect scores on all the tests. During meals at the officers' mess hall with classmates from the UK and around the world, he would expound on the lessons learned from the classic books *On War* by Carl von Clausewitz and *The Art of War* by Sun Tzu. Tal was surprised and disappointed that few fellow officers-in-training took the same interest.

Occasionally, Col. Kendrick "Kenny" Barnes, Defense Advisor to Jamaica's High Commissioner to Great Britain, would invite Tal and the other young Jamaican officers at Sandhurst to have dinner at his house. The Defense Advisor is equivalent to the senior military attaché at an embassy abroad, while the High Commissioner holds the same rank as an ambassador. These get-togethers presented an opportunity for the Jamaicans at Sandhurst to connect with a high-ranking officer while enjoying a Jamaican welcome far from home. Col. Barnes had a reputation for looking after the officers marked for higher leadership. The informal sessions also gave him a chance to evaluate them for future assignments in the esteemed Jamaica Defense Force, which has its own proud legacy.

The JDF descends directly from the British West India Regiment (BWI), which was formed in the 1790s to help protect British possessions in the Caribbean. Initially, the regiments were made of free and enslaved men, some of whom had fought as Loyalists on the British side in the American Revolution. The use of black soldiers in the West Indies was largely motivated by the huge losses of white British soldiers who died from yellow fever and malaria soon after arriving in the region. Soldiers of African descent had a much higher rate of survival and were thus seen as essential, despite reservations. The irony of arming the enslaved is not lost and mirrors the contradictory history of the Caribbean. Jamaican soldiers would distinguish themselves in many battles over the decades and be awarded three Victoria Crosses, the highest honor bestowed by the UK for bravery in action.

After Sandhurst, Tal joined the JDF helicopter unit and started pilot training with the Canadian Air Force in Manitoba. Upon completion, he was assigned to the JDF Air Wing at the Up Park Camp in Kingston. Tal shined in his new career flying Jet Ranger helicopters through Jamaica's thickly forested valleys and over high mountains. Sometimes he rescued stranded people, but most of the time, he and his crew searched for marijuana fields. At times, he would land his helicopter between trees right in front of the house of a surprised ganja grower. Tal had found his calling as a pilot, though he questioned the use of the military for what he considered to be police work, not national defense.

Back at the Kingston base, Tal took up football again, this time making the JDF team. JDF gave the good footballers plenty of time off from their military jobs to practice in the mornings and evenings. Unfortunately, as a helicopter pilot, Tal couldn't take advantage of the time off, so he could only practice when the schedule allowed. Nonetheless, he proved to be a solid player and kept in good shape while also pursuing a myriad of other interests, such as how food and vitamins affected the body. He never just dabbled in the subjects but immersed himself.

In the meantime, Leo had graduated from Sandhurst and went on to study aeronautical engineering at university. After that, he also joined the JDF Air Wing as a maintenance officer for helicopters and fixed-wing aircraft. Tal and Leo's paths crossed once again with their coincidental decision to join the JDF Air Wing, and the two became fast friends. Pride led Leo's maintenance unit to think of the helicopters as theirs and that they just lent them out for the pilots to fly. The prideful pilots, like Tal, saw maintenance as logistical support for their "tip-of-the-spear" front-line aerial mission. In practice, it was all good-natured banter that built an *esprit de corps* in the Air Wing.

Leo was as surprised as anyone that Tal had embarked on a JDF career, since he had not shown any interest at Calabar High School. However, he quickly recognized Tal's attention to detail, which tended to spill over into the obsessive compulsive. That was exactly the quality good helicopter pilots needed, especially when flying their aircraft dangerously close to the tops of trees over Jamaica's steep mountains looking for contraband. Tal soon got a reputation for doing everything well—a total perfectionist.

About this time, Tal's parents separated, which set them on a path to divorce. The two had never completely meshed, despite their attraction to each other. Their expectations in marriage radically differed, so much so that Blossom took pills to control depression. The time had come. Both had already begun to establish themselves independently as successful educators, which also meant Blossom had her own source of income. Once the children were old enough to be on their own, she got into her little Toyota Corolla, drove away, and never took another pill.

CHAPTER 6

G.I. JANE

On a lark, after a friend's dare, twenty-one year-old Denise Muir signed up for the 1979 Miss Jamaica Beauty Pageant. She had never entered a beauty pageant and really didn't know much about them. She didn't even think she was good-looking enough, but she was anxious to find out. At first, she had stage fright while practicing for the big night, but she conquered her fears and learned to connect with the audience and judges while walking with poise and grace. Despite her lack of experience, she came in 6th in the highly competitive contest and won the "Best Legs" award.

Soon after returning to her job in a bank, Denise saw one of her colleagues come to work wearing a JDF uniform. Intrigued, Denise asked what it was like to be a soldier. She liked what she heard about the mental and physical challenges. With some encouragement from her colleague, Denise, on a whim that would once again take her well outside her comfort zone, signed up for an officer candidate tryout. As it turned out, she was the only woman among 58 men aspiring to be officers. So the trainers put Denise, who was petite and only 5'3" tall, in the same class with them. She went through the same physical and mental tests and trials as her male counterparts, thus making her a real G.I. Jane.

For the rifle shooting test, she tied for first place out of the entire class. While most of the men washed out, Denise made it into the officer program. At her "Passing Out," or graduation ceremony, a Kingston newspaper found out that not only was she the only female in the class of officer candidates but that she had also been a Miss Jamaica contestant. It was an irresistible story. The headline read, "From Beauty Queen to Soldier."

When Denise reported to the JDF Training Depot in Newcastle, in the hills above Kingston, Tal had completed his basic officer training and had a couple of months of downtime before starting at Sandhurst. He took advantage of the time by enrolling in most of the training courses available at the base. One day he came across Denise, who appeared a bit overwhelmed with the demands and particularly worried about getting the right shine on her boots. Tal helped her and became quite attracted to the "badass" girl who had slogged out the tryouts with almost 60 men. He would leave encouraging notes in her locker, such as, "Stay positive. You got this!" They began seeing each other off and on, nothing too serious, and became good friends.

After Tal started at Sandhurst, Denise was selected for continued officer training in the UK at the Royal Air Force College in Cranwell, about two hours by train from Sandhurst. The two arranged to date on weekends by meeting halfway between their military schools in Grantham, Prime Minister Maggie Thatcher's hometown. Their daily per diem was so meager that they got together at the local McDonald's, where they could linger longer without spending much. They saw each other again in Jamaica and then Manitoba, where Denise also trained to be a pilot. During the Canadian winter, when the weather was too severe for flying, she and Tal took up weight lifting at the gym. Their JDF assignments regularly overlapped with a couple of months of lag time, just enough to keep the staggered long-distance relationship going.

Back in Jamaica, Denise had become buff enough that she decided to enter bodybuilding competitions, again on a whim. At her first event, members of the audience recognized her from the Miss Jamaica pageant a couple of years earlier. A few decided to have some fun at her expense by shouting out, "Hey, girl, you're in the wrong pageant!'

In 1985, after five years of on-and-off dating, Tal decided he liked Denise too much to be away and went to see her. When Tal arrived and told her how much he missed her, Denise took the initiative and said, "Well, why don't we get married? We do like each other and can't seem to stop seeing each other." Tal readily agreed to the proposal from the gutsy girl he admired so much and had fallen in love with. Denise understood Tal quite well, especially his restless drive to succeed at whatever task he took on. While she could not foresee him becoming a bobsledder, she sensed going into marriage that sooner or later, something would demand his full attention.

PART TWO:

A WILD IDEA

CHAPTER 7

AMERICAN DREAMERS

As Tal and Denise settled into marital life with steady jobs and promising futures, two Americans, William "Will" Maloney and George Fitch, found themselves in Jamaica casting about for a larger purpose. Both harbored illusory ambitions beyond their conventional employment. Will was a business manager in his late twenties, and George was nearly a senior federal civil servant in his late 30s. Little in their life trajectories suggested anything but continued modest career success, leading to comfortable obscurity as they passed through the phases of life. That surely would have been their fate had not a chance business connection brought them together.

Will grew up in an upper-middle-class family in Seattle, Washington, and loved watching the Winter Olympics on TV. He would choke up at the pageantry of the opening ceremonies and, for a magical moment, imagine himself there. Although an excellent skier, Will knew he would never be good enough to make the US Olympic team. But the yearning to make it to the Olympics never died. He just tucked it away.

While attending the University of San Diego, Will met and dated fellow student Teresa Issa, a Jamaican from a prominent family. By coincidence, Will had studied the Jamaican economy in one of his economics classes and learned quite a bit about the country. After Teresa returned to Jamaica and he to Seattle, they realized that their relationship would not last for long if they stayed apart. During one of their long-distance phone calls, they concluded they would either have to marry or break up. Will asked Teresa to hold the line while he stepped away to talk to his brothers, Tom and Ted, about what to do. They liked Teresa and the idea of her as a sister-in-law. Will got back on the phone line and asked Teresa if she would marry him. She said yes. They married six months later in Kingston.

In 1984, as Will was pursuing a career as a stockbroker with Dean Witter in Florida, he received a call from the head of Tropicana Energy in the US about setting up an ethanol-producing plant in Jamaica. Will had no intention of moving to Jamaica or getting into a business there. However, since he was already connected in Jamaica through Teresa and liked visiting the island, he agreed to take the job, but for only one year. The basic concept of the business was to import surplus wine spirits from France, Italy, and Spain and process them into fuel grade ethanol using an existing sugar mill. From there, the plan was to export the refined ethanol to the US to mix with gasoline.

Before leaving the US for Jamaica, Will watched the 1984 Winter Olympics in Sarajevo and let his imagination run free in the moment. While following the alpine events, he noticed a skier from Lebanon who skied no better than him. The International Olympic Committee's (IOC) policy of greater inclusiveness gave Lebanon and other countries with little exposure to the Winter Olympics a chance to enter an athlete, such as a skier, even if they were not ranked highly. In so doing, the IOC hoped to inspire more athletes from a broader range of countries to master sports they would not otherwise consider. Greater inclusion might also soften the image of the Olympic Movement as being elitist.

Will and Teresa leased a house in the upscale Stoney Hill section of Kingston. Their landlord, Mike Fennel, happened to be the president of the Jamaican Olympic Association. Will and Mike hit it off and became good friends. Thinking back to the Lebanese Olympic skier in Sarajevo, Will could not resist asking Mike if Jamaica would consider entering a good skier—perhaps himself—in the 1988 Winter Olympics in Calgary. As the spouse of a Jamaican, Will could qualify for Jamaican citizenship and, thus, could represent the country.

Mike made it clear that the Jamaican Olympic Association would only support athletes who were competitive, period. They were not going to waste resources on funding athletes just to participate, as this did nothing to promote the country or the sport. Jamaica, after all, had an enviable reputation and sterling image as a track and field powerhouse in the Summer Olympics since the late 1940s. The country's sports authorities were intent on protecting and nourishing that tradition.

The unambiguous dismissal by Mike might have been the end of it. Chastened but not defeated, Will considered other Winter Olympic sports where Jamaica could have an edge. He ran through the events with his brother, Tom, and they landed on bobsledding because success depended in part on good sprinters. A strong push at the top of the track usually determines who finishes first at the bottom. Indeed, in a sport where spots on the podium are decided by hundredths of a second, speed generated in what is known as the "fly zone" at the start, before the sledders hop into the sled, is an essential component of the sport. Will talked to Jamaican friends about the possibility of putting together a bobsled team in view of the country's outstanding sprinters, but no one had any interest. The whole idea was too foreign and too bizarre.

Will wasn't looking to try out as a bobsledder, but if a team was ever formed, he might just realize his personal wish to march in the opening ceremony as an official. In the meantime, Will had work to do in gearing up the ethanol plant for production. Crucially, he needed to ensure the ethanol produced met the requirements for sale in the United States without prohibitive tariff duties. His boss had already been in touch with the US Foreign Commercial Service headquarters in Washington, D.C., to see how they could tap into the Caribbean Basin Initiative (CBI). Set up by then-President Reagan, the goal of the CBI was to help developing countries like Jamaica increase exports and build a stable economy. Will's ethanol company looked to be a good CBI candidate. As the principal implementer of the CBI, George Fitch was the man to see.

*   *   *

As the offspring of three generations of Presbyterian missionaries in China, George had his own unique and exotic background that instilled in him a fearless *chutzpah* that anything was possible. His grandfather, George A. Fitch, lived in Nanking when Japanese forces took control of the city in 1937 and witnessed the atrocities first-hand. He took many risks to protect people in danger and document the horror that became known as the "Rape of Nanking." He even smuggled out pictures and film sewn into his jacket that he used in presentations across the US, calling attention to the crimes committed by the Japanese military.

As longtime foreigners in China—more than 75 years—the Fitch family spoke several Chinese dialects fluently, understood the culture well, and glided easily through Chinese power circles. The movers and shakers they associated with included General Chiang Kai-shek, leader of the Chinese Nationalist Forces, and his influential wife, Madame Chiang Kai-shek. Less is known about George's father, Albert C. Fitch, and his uncle, George Kempton Fitch, but they too may have played an active role in clandestinely opposing Japanese forces in China. Given their broad range of contacts and keen knowledge of the land and language, they would likely have been approached to work for the Flying Tigers, a group of mostly volunteer American aviators recruited to fly for China against the Japanese.

As the Chinese Communist forces under Chairman Mao Zedong consolidated control over most of the country, Albert Fitch moved with his pregnant wife and young children to Canton (Guangzhou) in the south, one of the last Nationalist strongholds in China. George was born there six weeks early, in December 1948, as the Communists attacked the city. The family fled again to the safer, British-controlled city of Hong Kong across the bay. From there, they made their way to India, where George's father began a new career. George's parents moved again to Singapore and enrolled him in the International American School. By then, George had learned to speak several Chinese dialects and had acquired French, Italian, and German.

At the international high school in Singapore, George excelled in tennis and swimming and continued competing in those sports after enrolling at the University of Singapore. In fact, he was so good at swimming that the Government of Singapore asked him to represent the country at the 1968 Summer Olympics. At the time, competing for a foreign country would require him to give up his US citizenship, which he was unwilling to do.

After completing two years of college in Singapore, George moved to the US to finish his bachelor's degree in economics and later earn an MBA from George Washington University (GW) in Washington, D.C. While teaching an introductory economics course at GW, one of the students in his class, Patricia Blazy, caught his eye. They would soon marry, and she would become his lifelong partner for 40 years, even when he left his safe and predictable government career to chase a most dubious dream.

George joined the US Foreign Commercial Service and rose through the ranks to be the face of the CBI. The timing for Will's ethanol processing plant seeking entry into the US perfectly aligned with George's assignment to the US Embassy in Kingston.

CHAPTER 8

CONCEPTION

Will and George hit it off right away, even though their temperaments differed—Will the more diplomatic and tactful, George the more brash, "let's get it done now" type. Both had the gift of supreme confidence and became tennis partners and drinking buddies. Like Will, George made friends easily in foreign countries and liked to think big. At 28, Will was the fitter of the two, as he continued to stay in good shape, even if the prospect of skiing in the Olympics receded. George, at 39, had become slightly pudgy and a chain smoker as his own athletic days had long faded. Still, he proved tough to beat in tennis and remained a strong swimmer. Once, George talked Will into joining him for a swim across part of Kingston Harbour, only to find out later that sewage had spilled into the water.

The two men loved the tropical lifestyle that Jamaica afforded them. Just about every American, as well as other foreigners working at embassies or in business, lived a more luxurious life than they could expect back home. That meant a big house surrounded by fragrant frangipani trees and bushes of bright red hibiscus flowers, sometimes with a splendid view of the bay. Homes almost always came with cooks, housekeepers, gardeners, and a driver. As for social life, the foreigners, largely Caucasian, mixed with their own kind while sprinkling in a few well-off, well-educated Jamaicans when hosting parties. Frequent partying was a way of life among the expats, as they usually had more time on their hands and plenty of booze on the counter.

At get-togethers without Jamaicans present, expats privately moaned to each other about everything wrong with Jamaica. The griping, tinged with a sense of superiority, mirrored the behavior of expats residing on all Caribbean islands. They never saw themselves as prejudiced, however, because they treated their house staff nicely and usually paid them better wages than they could get in the shanty towns where they lived. But a subtle and benign master-servant relationship from a bygone era continued to hold sway along with a bloated sense of privilege. The suffering and struggles of others far beneath them were unfortunate but unalterable facts of life and not supposed to intrude on their comfy lives—happily shallow and largely devoid of introspection.

A few foreigners, like Will and George, ran counter to the norm. While they both had a foot in the expat camp, their much wider circle of Jamaicans spanned the range from powerful politicians and successful businessmen to the proud farmer who hauled produce to market. Both moved with ease and confidence through the boisterous tumult of Jamaican society, and Jamaicans welcomed them. Through this lens, Will and George saw a richer, more enticing Jamaica. Open-air markets with ladies calling out deals from their stalls. The spicy aroma of jerk chicken mixed with the smoke of BBQs wafting through the air. The vibrations of boom boxes blasting reggae from shacks and bars, practically compelling the young and old to move in sync with the rhythm. The hustling, bantering, and bartering on every corner. Young men and women walking tall with a chip on their shoulder while looking you straight in the eye as equals or even better. All of it made the island come alive with laughter and sensuality, from the first rays of morning sunlight to well past the onset of darkness when a million brilliant stars splashed across a black Caribbean sky.

Will's marriage to Teresa gave him access to Jamaica's elite. But for Will to go beyond the family connection, he had to earn deeper acceptance by showing he cared enough to advance the country. He proved to be the real deal. The same held for George, whose post as a Foreign Commercial

Service officer attached to the US Embassy also provided him entrée across the social and economic spectrum. Anyone wanting to do business in the US coveted a contact like him. But that alone would not give him insider status and influence with Jamaicans beyond his work.

George brought something else with him to Jamaica. As an American who moved to the US after growing up in Asia for the first 20 years of his life, he was essentially an immigrant in his own country. His experiences from a young age of engaging naturally with cultures vastly different from the American way of life gave him an outsider's perspective. He observed from a distance and, blind to barriers, saw possibilities that most of his countrymen could not. That sharpened insight and social fluidity carried over to Jamaica and served him well wherever he went. He knew what buttons to push to get his way.

*　*　*

The 1980s also saw gang violence intensify in the Kingston shantytowns, which even spilled into finer neighborhoods. Ganja became an unwanted export that brought ruthless drug gangs into the US and other countries. At the same time, Jamaica had plenty to be proud of, starting with a remarkably diverse population that coexisted with hardly a hint of racial or religious conflict. While people of African descent made up most of the population, people of Chinese, Indian, Middle Eastern, and European origin, or a mix of any of these, identified fully as Jamaicans without the need to distinguish their ethnic origin with a hyphen.

Almost all had access to a quality education system that gave youngsters a solid foundation to reach higher. Indeed, Jamaica has long produced top doctors, lawyers, scientists, executives, educators, engineers, and artists. At the same time, innovative entrepreneurs, such as Butch Stewart, the founder of Sandals and Beaches, and John Issa, founder of SuperClubs, expanded tourism markets in Jamaica and across the Caribbean and re-defined a major industry.

A drive to succeed, coupled with intense competition in every aspect of society, was embedded in the culture. That tenacity also created many of the world's finest track and field athletes and some of the most brilliant musicians. Harry Belafonte first rose to the global stage with renditions of West Indian calypso, followed by reggae's off-beat staccato rhythm with stars like Bob Marley, Jimmy Cliff, Byron Lee, Pluto Shervington, and, of course, Peter Tosh, among many others. These accomplishments set Jamaica apart as a Caribbean country and forged a stronger national identity, a trait that other Caribbean islanders noticed and sometimes envied.

Still, Jamaica struggled in the 1980s. The promised prosperity and expanded opportunity following independence never came, except for a handful. Corruption stifled economic progress, which exacerbated poverty and fomented political strife. Getting ordinary things done, like a property registration or a driver's license, could be excruciatingly difficult and made more frustrating by an under-resourced bureaucracy. These shortcomings, of course, validated the observations of expats and gave them another reason to bellyache among each other with a sense of satisfaction before it was time to go home. Paradoxically, starting a new venture could be remarkably simple just because it had never been done, and nothing stood in the way, as Will and George would discover.

*　*　*

In 1986, the Foreign Commercial Service assigned George to a tour in Paris as the US liaison to the 1987 Paris Air Show. It was a big promotion, and George's wife, Patricia, very much looked forward to living in Paris. But after 12 years of government work, George was bored and, at times, disparaging of the stuffy Foreign Commercial Service. He felt ready to strike out on his own as an independent business consultant with a focus on the Caribbean region. He envisioned bouncing between homes in Washington, D.C., Jamaica, and Belize, all places where he had cultivated good political and business contacts who could be turned into well-paying clients. Despite a promising career with the Foreign Commercial Service and a plum assignment in Paris, he quit.

With a touch of cheeky humor that suited his feisty personality, George called his new consulting company "IOP Associates." The acronym IOP stood for "Instead of Paris." George's bailing on Paris, with all its charming cafes, striking landmarks, and magnificent museums, dismayed Patricia. She squarely blamed Will for George's decision, saying it ruined her life. She never forgave him.

Unsurprisingly, Will's company, Tropicana Energy, became one of George's first clients. With the ethanol plant up and running, Will needed to lobby the powers that be in Washington, D.C., to allow them to import the ethanol as a fuel additive and gain a foothold in the American market. George had the connections to negotiate the maze of regulations along with the moxie of a natural-born huckster to bust through roadblocks thrown up by big competitors. The direction of both their lives, as well as their fortunes, was about to take a dramatic turn.

The two men frequented a favorite watering hole called the Sea Witch, located in New Kingston, a well-off business district in the city. At the bar upstairs, Will typically ordered Red Stripe beers, while George preferred rum and cokes. It was a good place to meet after work or following a tennis game and shoot the breeze. One day, over drinks, Will decided to bounce off George the nagging notion of a Jamaican bobsled team that had stuck in his head, even though everyone else had dismissed it. Will explained his vision of tapping into Jamaican sprinting dominance that could be applied to pushing bobsleds. Without hesitation, George stood up, slammed his hand on the bar, and said, "We gotta make this happen!" A couple of drinks later, they had both committed to the outlandish scheme without really grasping the colossal challenge ahead.

While Will figured a bobsled team might just take him to the Olympics so he could walk in the opening ceremonies, George had his own personal ambitions. A worldly operator at odds with the temperament of a dedicated bureaucrat, he had always wanted to hatch an idea that could be turned into a movie. For both men, forming a Jamaican bobsled team had an element of satisfying personal aspirations as well as the thrill of creating something unheard of on a blank slate in Jamaica. It didn't matter that neither of them knew anything about bobsledding other than the fact that good sprinters should push bobsleds faster. Luckily for them, Jamaica fostered a culture of launching preposterous ideas, even in the face of doubters.

Bar patrons come up with exciting schemes to change the world all the time. As the creative juices flow, they furiously scratch their inspirations on paper napkins, only to be forgotten the next day when the alcoholic haze wears off. Not this time.

CHAPTER 9

WHO WANTS TO BE
A BOBSLEDDER?

The whole story is very unlikely . . .
It's just a very unlikely thing to have happened.

—Tal Stokes

George wasted no time. The day after the talk in the bar, he flew back to Washington, D.C., and cold-called Dave Heim, president of the United States Bobsled and Skeleton Federation (USBSF) in Lake Placid, New York. He asked Heim, out of the blue, if he would be willing to come to Jamaica and help select and train a Jamaican bobsled team for the upcoming 1988 Winter Olympics. Intrigued by the concept, Heim considered the unusual proposal for a brief moment before saying, "Yes!" It would not be the only time George would convince a stranger to support the Jamaican bobsledding quest.

George rang Will right away and shouted into the phone, "We're on!" and recounted the support expressed by Heim, who was well aware of Jamaica's great sprinters. In fact, Heim told George that the USBSF had already begun wooing top American football and track athletes, including Willie Gault and Willie Davenport, to take up the sport. Heim said he would bring with him to Jamaica William Napier, the Executive Director of the USBSF, another heavy hitter, to help out.

Heim and Napier could easily have blown off George's request to help select a Jamaican bobsled team to compete in the Olympics, which was only six months away. At this point, it was all still a fantasy. The fact that they agreed to come anyhow, however, speaks to their own self-confidence and openness to do something nuts and daring just because they could. Bobsledders tended to be like that.

While Heim and Napier wanted to help the Jamaicans become bobsledders, they had another motive they shared with George. The USBSF needed political support to crack the continental European domination of international bobsledding authority, then known as the *Féderation International de Bobsleigh et de Tobogganing* (FIBT). The US already had an alliance with Canada and Great Britain to challenge the block, but that was not enough to wrest control. Jamaican membership in FIBT would give them another friendly vote and improve their chances of taking over. The Jamaicans knew nothing about these power nuances at the time, but they picked up on the political game and would throw their support to the North American and UK challengers.

Heim also told George and Will that the IOC had recently voted to stagger the Winter Olympics and Summer Olympics two years apart, beginning in 1994. This meant that Jamaica would have the opportunity to enter teams in three Winter Olympics (1988, 1992, and 1994) over six years instead of eight. The compressed schedule would allow for more Olympic experience for the athletes at a lower cost. The fortuitous IOC decision prompted Will and George to start thinking about long-term development beyond 1988. The absence of a team, organization, sponsors, sleds, local approval, and any real knowledge of the sport did not deter them.

Will went back to Mike Fennel, the president of the Jamaica Olympic Association, and told him that the US Bobsled Federation was ready to send two top coaches from Lake Placid to Jamaica to evaluate potential bobsledders. He also noted the US Bobsled Federation was trying to bring on US sprinters to give the American teams an extra edge in the push at the start, thus strengthening the argument for recruiting Jamaican sprinters as bobsledders. Sensing Will and George's seriousness, as well as the focus on recruiting powerful runners, Mike came around, notwithstanding his earlier reservations.

In August, George and Will scheduled tryouts in early September in Kingston. They put up posters, bought radio time, and talked to track clubs but garnered almost no response. The whole concept seemed wholly foreign and alien. The lack of interest worried Will, as George had already secured a commitment from Heim and Napier to fly down, at their own expense, to evaluate the prospects for forming a team.

Will invited Mike over to his house with George to see what he could do to turn around the lack of interest, as time was getting short. Mike brought over Keith Shervington, the Secretary General of the Jamaica Olympic Association, to get his take. Keith suggested that Will and George meet with JDF Col. Ken Barnes—the same Col. Barnes who had been the Jamaican Defense Advisor in the UK when Tal was there—in hopes that he might be able to identify and encourage athletic soldiers who could qualify for training.

Within a couple of days, Keith had set up the meeting with Col. Barnes for Will and George to make their pitch. Col. Barnes listened intently. He already had quite an interest in world-top-level sports since his son, John Barnes, played in the English Premier League as a star footballer for Liverpool FC. As a senior officer with a military bearing that conveyed unmistakable authority, he wanted to know the specifics of what the sport entailed and what kind of athletes they needed. George and Will gave their now well-rehearsed presentation about how bobsled races were often won or lost depending on how fast a team pushed the sled at the start—hence the advantage of getting sprinters. Col. Barnes didn't laugh it off, as others had. Col. Barnes didn't take long to reflect on the audacious proposal and exclaimed, "I'm all in!" He called in Major George Taylor, who was in charge of JDF sports, to ask who might fit the requirements. Major Taylor suggested Lieutenant Devon Harris, a strong and outstanding middle-distance runner, and Private Michael White, the JDF's top sprinter.

Will and George also mentioned one more requirement to Col. Barnes. They would need a driver with outstanding hand-eye coordination who could steer the sled while speeding down a track at 80–90 miles an hour. Col. Barnes knew exactly the man for that—JDF Captain Dudley "Tal" Stokes. As the best helicopter pilot in the JDF, Tal had developed a keen sense for the nuances of manipulating a sophisticated machine that mimicked those of a bobsled pilot. Col. Barnes directed Major Taylor to notify Tal, Devon, and Michael to attend the tryouts, as well as put out a general notice to all JDF athletes for possible selection to be on the bobsled team. He even offered a conference room at the JDF base for an initial briefing.

Col. Barnes's decision to tap JDF athletic talent sharply buoyed the spirits of Will and George. As Will put it, "Col. Barnes was the most enthusiastic supporter we had or would encounter prior to the Olympics. If it wasn't for Mike, Keith, and Col. Barnes, nothing would have happened."

Tal, Devon, and Michael interpreted Col. Barnes's request to attend the bobsled try-outs as an order. They duly gathered, along with 30 other JDF members, as well as a few non-military athletes, to hear what Heim and Napier had to say about what it took to be a bobsledder. None of the Jamaicans knew anything about the sport, but they listened intently. About halfway through the session, George turned off the lights, and the American coaches played videos of bobsled races, including several showing vivid crashes. When the lights came on, most of the attendees decided they had seen enough and left. Some had actually sneaked out while the room was still dark. But Tal, Devon, and Michael stayed, though they too could probably have excused themselves, notwithstanding the request/order from their senior commanding officer.

The next day, at the National Stadium in Kingston, Heim and Napier put the remaining dozen candidates through a series of demanding physical and mental tests for evaluation. They used the same criteria for the Jamaicans as they did for prospective American bobsledders. Halfway through, Will asked Heim and Napier how it was going. They told him several of the candidates looked good, particularly Tal, who naturally took on the leadership role. He not only met the athletic requirements but also exhibited a maturity that some of the others did not have, even if they showed more athletic ability. Lt. Devon and Pvt. Michael had no problem meeting the criteria either. Michael tended to be quiet and deferential given his private rank, whereas Devon displayed more initiative befitting his officer status.

Devon grew up in the rough and violent ghetto of Kingston, called Waterhouse. It is part of a larger section of the city named Olympic Gardens for Jamaica's first Olympic sprinters, an irony not lost. Devon's family was so poor that he often went to bed hungry. His grandmother used to tell him stories about soldiers prevailing against all odds, and the theme resonated. A loner with few friends, Devon found school a safe haven from the gangs and gunshots, day and night, that cracked across the shanty town. Some classmates who had dropped out to stake out a street corner as their turf mocked him for studying hard.

Devon wasn't great at sports but did well enough in running track and playing soccer at school, usually barefoot, until he saved enough money to buy a pair of Converse tennis shoes. Once, a rival beat Devon badly in an 800-meter race. He was devastated to the point of crying but vowed to come back and beat him, which he did the following year. It was the only first place he ever got in track and field in school, but it was the only one that mattered. He never forgot that satisfaction.

After taking his "A" level exams and graduating from Ardenne High School in 1984, he lost his safe space and had to face the harsh and often scary reality of the "hood." Still recalling his grandmother's soldier stories, he signed up for the grueling selection process to be a JDF officer. Being a good athlete with a scholastic foundation gave him an edge in making it to the final selection stage, where all aspiring officers had to give a speech. His topic was the importance of sports in his life. He practiced hard and aced the presentation that earned him the nod for officer training. The gift of speaking, as well as athletics and learning, would serve him well later in life as a motivational speaker. But for now, he just wanted to be a good soldier. Like Tal, he was also selected for advanced training at Sandhurst and came back to Jamaica as an infantry lieutenant.

Two civilians, Sammy Clayton and Caswell Allen, met the physical and mental criteria as well, but just barely. Sammy, a railway worker by day and a sound engineer/music producer by night, came across to George and Will as a bit geeky-looking, not what a bobsledder should look like. However, as with Tal, he demonstrated excellent hand-eye coordination skills, which tagged him as a potential driver. Coincidentally, Caswell had attended Ardenne High School with Devon.

Freddie Powell showed up halfway through the trials, claiming that he had to catch different buses from his hometown in the country town of Junction of St. Elizabeth Parrish. As he was pushing 40 years old, Will, George, and the coaches wondered if he would make it through the tests. Though he was not a true athlete who had mastered a sport, he still showed raw strength and athleticism. Wearing bright red socks and black Converse loafers, Freddie stood out as the most colorful personality at the tryouts, and he carried himself with a gentle but unmistakable confidence. Although he hadn't played organized sports like the others, Freddie proved to be ox-strong from working on local farms. He made a little extra money as a part-time electrician and guitar player with a flair for reggae. In the end, the American coaches selected Tal, Devon, Michael, and Sammy to form the core of the team. Freddie and Caswell would be alternates.

For Tal, the idea of driving a finely tuned racing machine fast down a sheet of ice perfectly appealed to his nature. He quickly saw how bobsledding married technology with physicality, very much like piloting a helicopter up and down mountains. Although training as a bobsledder would take him away from flying helicopters, he decided to give it a shot. In the group of team finalists, Tal saw himself as the team captain since he was the ranking officer and naturally took charge. Each man selected had proven to be a good enough athlete for competitive bobsledding, though some were better than others. All of them brought personal baggage that would test the team as much as the training and competition over the next few months and years.

CHAPTER 10

NOW WHAT?

George and Will had done it. They had their Jamaican Bobsled Team, with six guys signed on. The only thing left was to get them to the Olympic Games five months away, even though none of the six had seen or touched a bobsled, much less gone down a track. They didn't even have a coach who could teach them how to bobsled, one of the most dangerous sports in the world, nor did they have any money to pay for what also happens to be one of the most expensive sports in the world. Then there was the matter of actually qualifying for the Olympics.

Seeing the potential for publicity early on, the Jamaican Tourist Board wrote a modest US $10,000 check for the team. The Tourist Board liked the idea of a feel-good story about a Jamaican bobsled team to deflect the bad publicity from Jamaican drug gangs. Appleton Rum also provided some funding that made it the official drink of the bobsled team. While encouraging, the total contributions amounted to about 1% or 2% of the budget of a top European team contender.

An anxious realization swept over Will and George that the team might not even make it to the starting blocks without a lot more cash. Keeping their anxiety in check, they reached out to P.C. Harris, a well-known Jamaican publicist, about marketing and promoting a bobsled team starting from nothing and aiming to reach the Olympics. P.C., who also happened to produce music, movies, and TV and radio shows, immediately saw the potential for a Jamaican bobsled team and readily agreed to help. He engaged his art director, Frenchman Pierre Lamaire, to design a logo of bobsledders with a tropical theme. Pierre created a captivating picture of bobsledders tearing down a green slope to a beach lined with palm trees with the slogan invented by P.C.: "The Hottest Thing On Ice." Sun Island, a local T-shirt printer, was contracted to produce several hundred T-shirts with the logo that George figured he and the team could sell to raise money.

As P.C. looked at all the angles to generate publicity, he decided that the team should have its own song and collaborated with Jamaican musician Peter Couch to write one with a catchy reggae beat. The aim was to capture the singular, if not bizarre, quest of Jamaican bobsledders heading to the Olympics. Together, they came up with "Hobbin' and a Bobbin," also known as the *Jamaican Bobsled Theme Song*. P.C. and Peter engaged performer Bob Andy as the lead vocalist with a band P.C. brought together that he called The Ragamuffins. They produced a 45 RPM vinyl record (now found on YouTube).

> *A doo-wop, a doo-wop, slip, slip, slide*
> *Bob, bob, bobbin, bob, bob bobsleigh*
> *Jamaica bobsleigh. Yeah!*
> *In a Sunday down south, tropical isle*
> *Beautiful, warm, Jamaica style*
> *We've been training, gaining*
> *Straining and feigning but we ain't complainin'*
> *Jamaica bobsled*

The punchy public relations initiative soon sparked the notion that maybe a Jamaican bobsled team could emerge as an uncommon branding opportunity. The incongruity of Black men from a tropical country racing bobsleds on ice in the Winter Olympics certainly got everyone's attention. P.C. Harris had laid the foundation and sown the seeds, but, until money flowed, the bulk of the cash would have to come out of Will and George's pockets—a lot more than they had reckoned.

Meanwhile, Will tended to the corporate details by formally registering the Jamaica Bobsled Federation as an official Jamaican sporting organization. He became its first president. Mike and Keith smoothed the way for the new federation to be accredited by the Jamaica Olympic Association, which enabled them to apply for membership in the FIBT. Once accepted by the FIBT, they would be eligible to compete and qualify for the Olympics as bobsledders. At the time, they just needed to enter and finish one World Cup bobsled competition. To keep costs down, Will and George opted to compete only in the two-man sled, as it was cheaper and less difficult than the four-man sled. A few things began falling into place—a team ready to roll, official paperwork, an inviting image, and even a few bucks. Still, one nagging reality remained for the Jamaicans: actually climbing into a real bobsled and learning how to slide down an ice track really fast instead of just watching videos about it.

CHAPTER 11

FROM PASTIME DIVERSION TO HIGH-TECH EXPANSION

R acing sleds down a hill began sometime in the 1870s in the mountain resort village of St. Moritz, Switzerland, as well as in the lumber towns of upstate New York near Lake Placid. No one knows for sure which location was first or if one location influenced the other. The sport may have sprung up independently in each place. We do know more about the sledding origins in St. Moritz, where a local hotelier, Caspar Badruft, began promoting his inn, the Palace Hotel, as a winter vacation destination. He had already attracted a well-to-do British clientele during the summer months. He just needed to convince them to experience a snowy wonderland so he could keep the hotel open all winter as well. The prospect of amusing diversions with plenty of alcohol and good food took hold. Soon enough, St. Moritz became a fashionable holiday escape from the gray monotony of the English winter.

While searching for recreation (alpine skiing had not yet been introduced), some of the Brits noticed the wooden sleds used by delivery boys to move them and their baggage from the train station to the hotel over snow-packed roads. Naturally enough, guests asked, "Why not borrow them and slide down a hill for a cheap thrill?" Before long, the visitors began racing each other through the streets of St. Moritz. Back then, four or five people would pile onto a sled and then move themselves from side to side, which caused their heads to "bob" back and forth. People watching called the new sledding enthusiasts "bobsledders," and the name stuck.

Often drunk and unable to steer, the out-of-control sledders collided with pedestrians, causing injuries and fueling local complaints. To get better control, the sledders attached two sleds together and installed a crude steering wheel connected to movable front runners. This technical improvement did allow the bobbing tourists to better operate the sleds as they descended, but it also enabled them to go faster, which caused the drivers to lose control when they hit higher speeds. That led to more severe crashes, injuries, and local outrage.

To avoid the ire of the townsfolk and the risk of banning bobsledding, which became a staple entertainment that generated a healthy tourism income, Badruft built a dedicated track at his own expense. The course, essentially a packed ice path with sharp curves lined with snowbanks on either side, ran from St. Moritz to the town of Cresta, slightly more than one kilometer farther down the mountain. Bobsledding guests loved the track made exclusively for them, and it kept them off the streets. The first organized competition on this "natural" track called the "Cresta Run" began in 1898, with teams usually consisting of three men and two women.

The popularity of bobsled competition on a track expanded to other alpine countries, such as Germany, Austria, France, and Italy, but the emerging sliding sport was still largely confined to those with means. At the first Winter Olympic Games in 1924 in Chamonix, France, the two-man bobsled became one of the five sports entered in the event. Only men could compete, despite the tradition of including women. The sleds started from a stationary position on an incline. A race official would remove a restraining pole holding the sled back so it could start sliding down the chute, slowly at first, before gaining speed. These conditions favored heavy men who could simply sit behind and let their weight increase the momentum of the bobsled. As with the recreational sledders before them, the racers would bob their heads and bodies back and forth to accelerate more quickly.

In these early years of Olympic and international competition, bobsledding attracted a colorful cadre of convivial, derring-do upper-class amateurs but not much athleticism. Gradually, bobsledding began winning over a few real sportsmen among the social elite, the most prominent and accomplished one being American Eddie Eagan. Before joining the four-man bobsled team (which had been added to the two-man team event) at the 1932 Olympics in Lake Placid, Eagan already had a string of remarkable accomplishments. He had graduated from Yale University, served as an artillery officer in France in World War I, graduated from Harvard Law School, was named a Rhodes Scholar to study at Oxford University, and won a gold medal in boxing (light heavyweight) at the 1920 Summer Olympics in Antwerp.

When a member of the 1932 US four-man bobsled team dropped out at the last minute, the head of the US Olympic Bobsled Committee—a good friend of Eagan's—asked if he would step in as a pusher. A competition should have been held to fill the empty spot, but because of the warm weather in Lake Placid, there was no time. So, Eagan, a natural athlete but with hardly any bobsled experience, joined the team at age 34 and helped the US team win a gold medal. The achievement made Eagan the only person to have won a gold medal in the Summer and Winter Olympics in a different sport.

In the early 1950s, bobsled racing dramatically changed from a risky pastime to a truly athletic sport that demanded speed, strength, and agility but remained just as dangerous. The FIBT started by implementing weight limits on sleds, which removed the benefit of recruiting the beefiest sledders. The FIBT also eliminated the stationary start and required teams to push the sled at the start and then jump on as it gathered speed.

Evolving regulations further stipulated that the sled be set against starting blocks with a 15-meter "fly zone" from where the teams would begin the push. At the 15-meter mark, the timing eye starts the clock once the nose of the sled breaks the beam. From there, the "start zone" extends for another 50 meters, where a second timing eye measures the push speed.

The purpose of the second timing eye is solely to note the speed of the push over the 50-meter distance and allow sledders and coaches to better understand performance at the crucial push stage. The total time is measured from the point where the bobsled breaks the beam after the first 15 meters to breaking the timing eye at the bottom finish line.

Near the end of the start zone, when the sledders have accelerated the sled and gravity takes over completely as the incline steepens, the team leaps in. The pilot jumps in first, followed by the pusher/brakeman, for a two-man sled. In the four-man sled, the driver hops in first and is followed by the second and third pushers on either side of the sled. Finally, the pusher/brakeman hops in at the back. The term "brakeman" is somewhat of a misnomer because the brakeman does not apply the brake during the race, only when the sled has crossed the finish line.

In the 1960s, artificial bobsled tracks made of reinforced concrete with built-in refrigerated coils began to replace natural tracks, which were dependent on outside temperatures to keep the ice and snow from melting. The FIBT required the ice to be kept at a constant temperature of precisely −11°C (12.2°F) from top to bottom. The reliably iced track allowed bobsledders to train more consistently over a longer season. Refrigeration also provided racers with more similar ice conditions. However, refrigeration reduced, but did not do away with, the ice temperature fluctuations typical of natural tracks when weather conditions changed. Out of tradition, only the original track of the Cresta Run in St. Moritz remains natural. This natural track served as the bobsled venue when St. Moritz hosted the Winter Olympics in 1928 and 1948.

More FIBT rules limited the artificial track length between 1200 and 1650 meters with 15 to 20 curves at a maximum gradient of 12%. Since each track has a different length and different numbers and types of curves, the home team always has a distinct advantage by getting in far more practice runs than any visiting team. Indeed, some tracks restrict training by visitor teams so they don't get too familiar with the track and beat the home team.

As soon as one team clears the track at the bottom, officials set off a buzzer, giving the next team at the starting block a 60-second window to begin their push. If a team is not present with their sled at the starting block or if the team fails to break the beam of the timing eye within the 60-second window, they are automatically disqualified. At the World Cup level, these start errors rarely occur because of the highly regimented routines that athletes undertake to prepare for their runs. Indeed, getting the logistics right is a crucial part of the race. One small mistake can quickly end the race for a team that may have trained for months and spent hundreds of thousands of dollars.

The best sledders will complete a run in just under a minute. The top teams in medal contention are often separated by just a few hundredths of a second. It's a cruel sport demanding perfection. The tiniest deviation in the push or the driving can knock a good team off the podium.

FIBT's biggest challenge has always been regulating technical enhancements of the sled to increase speed. It's a game of playing catch-up with technological innovations referred to as "sports engineering" or, more sinisterly, "technology doping." Of all the sled adjustments that have caused the most controversy, the heating of the runners to minimize friction with the ice stands out.

In the old days, teams regularly applied a blow torch to their steel runners just before the start that let them glide faster over the ice, and it was legal. The FIBT prohibited the practice and instituted strict temperature measurement protocols before each race. Officials use a "reference runner," which is exposed to the open air at the start house for one hour before the race, to establish a reference temperature. As the sleds are positioned in the "staging area" at the top, officials apply a sensor gauge to each runner. The sled runner temperature cannot exceed the temperature of the reference runner by more than 4°C.

If the temperature on any runner falls outside the variance, a second check is made. If the sensor still shows a variance greater than 4°C, the team is disqualified and there is no appeal. Bobsledders are allowed to polish their runners to remove water droplets or debris as well as make them smoother. But sledders cannot coat the runners. Special wooden or metal runner protectors or covers called "scabbards" are applied immediately after each run to ensure the runners don't get scratched.

In bobsledding, skirting the boundaries of the rules or evading them altogether and hoping to get away with it has almost become a sport in itself. A US team once rubbed banana peels on the rails to go faster, which didn't work and was likely illegal anyhow. More often, bobsled teams will warm the runners to be as close to the 4°C maximum variance as possible, even using electric blankets over the runners to keep them warm until testing. This requires extreme precision by technicians and frequent testing by the team to ensure none of the runners exceeds the limit.

Sometimes, it's not always the sled that is manipulated. Technicians managing the refrigeration unit cooling a track have been suspected of deliberately adjusting the temperature of the ice. Allowing the ice temperature to rise just a little above – 11°C for a short period can be enough to slow a particularly fast visiting opponent and give the home team another advantage.

Like many other sports, bobsledding has never been a level playing field, even when playing by the rules. In fact, improving bobsled performance has mushroomed into a high-tech industry with innovative sled design breakthroughs and new applications, all targets of espionage by opposing teams. Top teams today employ full-time engineers, computer scientists, and software designers. Enhancement of athlete performance receives just as much attention, as teams hire sports psychologists, nutritionists, medical specialists, and "bio-mechanists" (people who study the movements of athletes). The vast disparity between well-funded, cutting-edge European teams out to win medals and the barely-scraping-by Jamaicans would soon become glaringly clear. If bobsledding started out as a rich man's diversion a century earlier, it had expanded into a wealth-driven enterprise with million-dollar sponsorships by the time the Jamaican team entered the fray, selling T-shirts to raise money.

CHAPTER 12

BUMPY BEGINNING

We created quite a stir on the military helicopter tarmac right in the heart of Kingston, with cars stopping to see what was going on. But we worked every day to perfect the start. What we never did, however, is drive a push cart down a hill as portrayed in Cool Runnings. *Steering a bobsled is nothing like steering a push cart, so that exercise would have been pointless. For that, we needed to go down a real bobsled run.*

—Tal Stokes

With the nearest bobsled track 1500 miles due north, the Jamaican bobsled team needed something closer to home to train on while figuring out how to get on a track. Before returning home after recruiting the Jamaican team, American coaches Heim and Napier recommended making a metal sled on wheels to practice pushing. Jamaica had nothing like that, so the coaches gave Will the schematics to build one that resembled a four-man sled. He asked a couple of his mechanics at the ethanol plant to weld one together, which they did in 24 hours. At least the new Jamaican bobsled team had something that mimicked the essential push start with push bars, and they began practicing three hours a day during the weekdays and six hours on Saturdays for a month.

The team became quite good at pushing and developed good timing for jumping into the sled while going fast. But time was running out for them to have the chance to slide down a proper bobsled course under the guidance of a coach. George reached out to one of the most respected bobsledders in America, a big bear of a man named Howard Siler. As a former US Olympic bobsledder (1972, 1980), nine-time US champion, a bronze medalist in the world championships (1979), and a coach for the US national bobsled team in 1985, Howard had all the credentials. In 1980, the Washington Post quoted Howard, with a touch of gallows humor, "You know, they say a bobsled driver can't ask for much in life. When you jump in that seat, you only know two things for certain: The traffic's all one-way. And if you crash, at least you won't burn."

Having grown up in Lake Placid, Coach Howard, like all young men living in the Adirondacks area of upstate New York, had plenty of exposure to winter sports, including bobsledding. In fact, Lake Placid had the only bobsled track in North America at the time. Howard took to bobsledding naturally and had a drive to succeed. In his case, some early resentment seems to have been a motivator. In the late 1950s and 1960s, up-and-coming young bobsledders like Coach Howard typically came from blue-collar families and had to carve out time from school and work to squeeze in practice. The military bobsledders from nearby Air Force and Navy bases, however, were able to train nearly full-time on the track. Coach Howard hated their unfair advantage, so he set out to kick their butts.

Kicking butts made him into a champion bobsledder and may well have connected him better to the aspiring Jamaicans, who also had little time and no money compared to the well-funded national teams of other countries. Coach Howard needed to make a living, however, and asked for a $30,000 fee. George talked him down to a $5000 flat fee plus $2000 for every team they beat in Calgary to add some incentive. Howard agreed.

In late September 1987, Tal, Michael, Devon, Sammy, and Freddie flew to Lake Placid for what they thought would be their first chance to experience barreling down the chute in a bobsled. They got a good look at the Mt. Van Hoevenberg Olympic Bobsled Run, but the track had not yet been iced and so couldn't be used. Coach Howard could only work with them on how to push and load a bobsled on the local ice rink, the same one where the US hockey team had beaten the Soviet players in the 1980 "Miracle on Ice." He started by teaching the Jamaicans how to run on ice using special shoes with spikes to replicate a start and then watched them slip and slide all over before finding their balance.

Coach Howard also took the team for walks up and down the track so they could see the big curves and start to get a feel for the sport. He often had them over to his house for drinks and BBQ. These get-togethers gave the coach a chance to size up the character of the team members out side of practice, particularly after his students had a few drinks. The drinks inspired a festive mood at the house parties and, on occasion, sparked passionate discussions, usually initiated by Tal, the team's intellectual. All the Jamaicans passed the coach's drinking test, even if they weren't able to slide on a bobsled.

Unwilling to wait for the Lake Placid track to be iced, Howard arranged to fly the team to Calgary so they could finally get on a bobsled course. It also happened to be the course purpose-built for the upcoming 1988 Winter Olympics. Called the Winsport Canada Olympic Park, the track cost $27 million, which made it the most expensive and the most advanced in the world at the time. As with all modern bobsled tracks (also used for luge and skeleton sled competitions), this one was constructed using reinforced concrete with refrigerated cooling coils. The track measured 1494 meters, a little short of 1 mile, and consisted of 19 curves. The toughest and most dangerous part of the course was curve 8. Named the "Kreisel" (German for "gyro"), it wound around 360° and severely tested every driver sliding through it. Only a handful of bobsled tracks in the world incorporated this tricky turn.

A new team doesn't just start at the top of the course. That's too dangerous. So instead, they begin at the bottom quarter of the track, called the "Junior Start," to get a feel for how the bobsled moves as it gains speed through a few curves. Once comfortable, they start halfway up the track, then three-quarters. When ready, they push from the top.

Howard knew his sport, and the Jamaican athletes respected him. He found them a two-man sled to borrow and taught them the nuances of pushing for an explosive start and then jumping in quickly and orderly when the sled had gained enough speed. Once in the "hull" of the sled, Howard taught the Jamaicans how to tuck tightly together, forming a straight line of heads that should not move (unlike early bobsledders who deliberately "bobbed" their heads).

Tal learned the exacting art of steering using two ropes, each with a D-ring handle attached to a steering bolt in the front of the frame that moved the runners left and right. (The initial steering wheel used on bob-sleds in the first Winter Olympics had long been discarded.) Sammy also showed aptitude for driving a sled and trained as a pilot alongside Tal. Ideally, a driver tries to steer the sled as little as possible and instead lets the sled run "down the line" for the optimal zone along the bank of the curve to maximize speed. Thus, while hand-eye coordination is important, getting a "feel" for the sled ranks higher.

Tal inadvertently found out the importance of feel the first time he piloted the sled from the top of the course. He had always kept his helmet loose, which worked fine for slower runs from lower starting points on the track. From the top, however, the sled gained much more speed along with more rattling and G forces and shook the helmet loose. By turn four, the helmet had come down over Tal's eyes, making it nearly impossible to see the track. Still, he managed to make it down without flipping the sled. As Tal would learn over the next few years, sensing the G-force pressure points through one curve served to guide him to the next one. He purpose-fully developed "tunnel vision" while driving, like a horse with blinders, so that he would steer less and feel more.

Teams usually only get in a few practice runs a day. That's partly because it takes a lot of time to load a sled onto the back of a U-Haul-looking truck and drive it back to the top of the track for another run. The other reason is that bobsledders, particularly beginners, get banged around so much while hurling down the chute, even if they don't crash. Heads, limbs, and torsos can only take so much beating.

The Jamaicans crashed frequently and often had to be taken to the Foothill Hospital in Calgary for treatment and observation. Tal pushed through all the injuries, anxious and thrilled to get back on the track. Just as he imagined back in Jamaica, piloting a bobsled perfectly fit his love of manipulating machines and integrating himself into them. The skills of flying a helicopter synched with driving a bobsled, except bobsledding demanded more.

Since a full run (without crashing) lasted only a minute or less, actual sliding practice on a track might come down to just five minutes for a day, less than that for a harder and more unforgiving course, like the one in Lake Placid. The head rattling that bobsledders experienced on each run made it impossible to repeat exercises again and again all day. Over the course of a season, a seriously competitive bobsled team might get in merely 120–160 minutes of time on the ice.

To make up for the lack of actual on-the-track practice, bobsledders, particularly the East Germans, would spend hours visualizing the course from start to finish. Tal had already practiced visualizing almost anything he set his mind to, so this aspect came naturally. His visualization talent would prove crucial in the years ahead, as the team's perennial lack of funds only allowed them half the ice time of other teams, about 60–80 minutes a year. Tal's ability to see in his mind every nuance of racing down the chute would keep Jamaicans in the game.

CHAPTER 13

BARELY HANGING ON

Coach Howard liked the Jamaicans and their easy-going, fun-loving nature. In particular, he respected how seriously they took learning to be bobsledders. Howard would later tell his wife that the Jamaicans had more heart and soul than any athlete he had ever coached. While Coach Howard appreciated the drive and determination of the Jamaicans and wanted to keep coaching them, he also had a full-time job back in New York selling insurance. It has never been made clear if the coaching "contract" between Howard and George ever actually went into effect, was modified, or cancelled. In any case, Coach Howard had financial obligations of his own that overrode coaching.

After a few weeks of training the team in Calgary, Coach Howard called George, who was in Dallas, to let him know he would be flying back to New York. Just before leaving, the coach drove the van with the team and bobsled back up the hill for a last run. Along the way, he recognized a young bobsledder, Pat Brown, who was walking down the hill. Howard had long been a friend of Pat's family, who was also from the Lake Placid area. He stopped and introduced Pat to the Jamaican team. Pat had tried out for the 1988 US Olympic four-man bobsled team, but his team didn't make it, though he and the others were slated as Olympic alternates. With his prospects for racing in the Olympics dashed, Pat decided to drive out to Calgary, where he had an uncle he could stay with, and see what he could do to be part of the scene at the Winter Olympics.

At the age of 21, Pat had three years of bobsledding experience but had never competed internationally. Sensing an opportunity to keep the Jamaican bobsled momentum going without his presence, Howard asked Pat if he would be willing to help the Jamaican team. Pat readily agreed. However, his youth and relative inexperience didn't sit well with the Jamaicans, especially after having been coached by a world-class pro like Howard. Nonetheless, the team could use someone like Pat. He knew a lot more about bobsledding than they did, and he was willing to help coach and manage the team for free. The Jamaicans were in no position to be choosy. Fortunately, during that uncertain period, Pat proved to be a steady rock who came through for the team.

As it turned out, Howard had applied to be a "juror" for the upcoming Winter Olympic Games. This meant he would be one of the key officials monitoring the bobsled races to ensure fairness and rule compliance in a sport notorious for skirting the rules. As such, he would be a neutral party and not be able to coach—at least not openly.

Meanwhile, George made plans to head up to Calgary the next day after talking to Coach Howard about preparing the next steps for additional training and entering a qualifying race. The next day turned out to be October 19, 1987, Black Monday, the worst American stock market crash since the Great Depression. George happened to be heavily invested in the market and lost most of his fortune. Will, still in Jamaica, took a hit as well. Funding now would be even more constrained and might have left the team's future in doubt. Notwithstanding the blow to their wealth, however, neither George nor Will wavered in their commitment to see the Jamaicans in the Winter Olympics. They were both all-in, even if they had to dig deeper into their pockets.

The top priority now was to fly the team to Europe for the last Olympic bobsled qualifying event in late December in the tiny Tyrolean village of Igls, Austria. The Igls track, just a few miles outside Innsbruck, was one of the best in the world. It also happened to have a "Bob School," which the Jamaicans badly needed since they had only completed four runs from the top of the Calgary track.

George, Will, and Tal made a quick and essential decision to send everyone to Igls a month in advance of the competition. That allowed for a week of bobsled school and three weeks of training sessions on the track. Practicing sledding on the same track could give Team Jamaica a realistic chance.

At the time, the FIBT applied vague and loose qualifying requirements. With only a handful of countries in the world having a national bobsled team, there was never a need to limit or qualify teams. Still, the FIBT decided the Jamaicans had to compete in one race and make it down the track through four heats without crashing. Then they could become Olympians in the two-man bobsled and race in Calgary.

If the two Jamaican teams did not make it through all four heats at the World Cup in Igls, all the money Will and George had spent would have been wasted. All the convincing promises to the skeptical Jamaica Olympic Association members about fielding a competitive team for the Winter Olympics would become an embarrassment. And all the preparation and training the Jamaican bobsledders had gone through would be for naught.

CHAPTER 14

QUALIFY OR GO HOME

It wasn't much fun, and there wasn't much laughter. I personally was very driven because I recognized the kind of mountain that was in front of me. So, I was not particularly nice to the rest of the team. As far as I was concerned, I was the ranking officer, and I needed to get things done.

—Tal Stokes

N o one had really thought through how expensive the training and travel would be just to reach the qualifying race in Igls, which only became more problematic after Will and George had taken a hit in the stock market crash. In anticipation of a financial shortfall, George had asked a printing company in Kingston to produce several hundred Jamaican bobsled T-shirts that the team could stuff into their suitcases before leaving and sell if they needed to.

In order to pay for the airline tickets to Munich, Germany, Will tapped his brother Tom, who worked at their mom's travel agency in Seattle. Mom was a little surprised that the agency was buying the tickets on credit with only the vague promise of being repaid sometime down the road. Mom went along anyhow, even if she was not convinced the agency would ever see the money. Over the next four months, the travel costs for Tal, Devon, Michael, Sammy, and Freddie, as well as Pat, would come to over $38,000.

George arranged for the smallest rental car available in Munich, a Panda Fiat. At first, the guys looked at the car and wondered how six of them and all the luggage would fit. Somehow, they crammed in with their belongings for the two-and-a-half-hour drive to Igls. They checked into the hostel, Landesportheim, that was associated with the Igls bobsled school run by Sepp Haidacher, a well-known figure in the bobsledding world. Sepp's time would come to take Jamaican bobsledders to the next level, but not yet.

The track in Igls, officially named the Olympic Sliding Centre or Olympia Eiskanal Innsbruck, was first built as a natural track for the two-man bobsled world championship in 1935. Several bobsledders were killed in that first competition, causing officials to close it for modifications to make it less dangerous. When the International Olympic Committee (IOC) selected Innsbruck as the venue for the 1964 Olympics, the Austrians constructed a modern concrete track with built-in refrigeration. Even that state-of-the-art track didn't eliminate serious injuries in its first pre-Olympic competition.

The track again became the venue for bobsledding in the 1976 Winter Olympics when the IOC awarded Innsbruck the Games for the second time. The IOC had originally selected Denver to host the Games in 1976, but the city's inability to raise sufficient funds caused it to pull out. Hosting two Winter Olympics, plus numerous World Cups and World Championships, helped plant Igls on the map as a world-class training center.

The Jamaicans benefited immensely from the week of training at the Bob School. To keep going, they needed to find a two-man sled to train on but had no money to buy one. When they saw a beat-up sled on the side of the track, unclaimed by anyone, Tal made a command decision to take it. Nobody seemed to miss the apparently abandoned sled, so it was theirs to keep.

As in Calgary, the team started lower down the track at a point called *damen,* or "ladies," before working their way up. With the experience they had gained in Calgary and the Bob School, the team moved quickly to start at the top. The track was actually a little easier than the one in Calgary, and that allowed them to find their zone with less risk. But they still continued to crash.

Unfortunately, after Bob School, the Jamaican team got track training time only at night under lights when the temperatures dropped well below freezing. The major national teams had already reserved slots well in advance for training during the day. Sliding down ice in the cold of night made the runs much tougher. Moreover, their bodies consumed more calories in the colder temperatures, which meant the team had to eat even more. And this further stretched the per diem George had given them. That's when they pulled out the T-shirts from their suitcases and began selling them on the sidewalks. The curious and usually supportive Austrians initially thought the Jamaicans were American basketball players and were delightfully surprised to see black bobsledders. The number of T-shirts the Jamaicans sold during the day determined the quality of dinner they would have after practice that night.

Initially, the team subsisted on meals of bread and peanut butter. When Pat found an inexpensive Chinese restaurant that provided more food for the money, it became their go-to place when T-shirt sales were brisk. George arrived in Igls halfway through training to check on things. At Pat's forceful urging, bordering on confrontation, George upped the per diem for food so the team could get more calories.

All through training, the team still fumbled with the equipment while trying to follow bobsled practice protocols and managing limited track time. At Calgary, fewer teams gave them space to prepare for each run. At Igls, however, the Jamaicans had to deal with a host of very experienced teams with tight schedules. These teams didn't hold back on voicing their frustration with the Jamaican newbies and often shouted out, "Get better organized!" or "Get out of the way!" The Jamaican team's crashes, typically by flipping the sled on the side, further added to the delays and annoyances and indicated to the pros that they weren't ready.

The crashes sent all of the team members, at one time or another, to the local hospital. But they always got back on the track, except for Freddie. Freddie jumped in for a couple of runs and decided that was enough for now. Though Freddie was a superb athlete, he didn't have the same motivation as the others to speed down a track. Everyone liked him, though, because he brought a distinctive Jamaican country flavor to the team, even if he, unlike them, lacked the determination to be a bobsledder. Overall, morale was good despite the frequent hand-to-mouth existence and the stresses of trying to learn a new sport.

As the Jamaicans improved, the other teams observed their dedication and occasionally gave them tips on how to get better. Still, with few exceptions, they remained outliers among the international bobsled community. One notable exception was Prince Albert of Monaco, who was also training for his own Olympic debut in Calgary and was himself a bobsledder newbie. Impressed with the team's commitment, despite their small budget and willingness to take themselves out of their tropical comfort zone, he personally bought 50 T-shirts. That brought in badly needed cash for better food and lifted spirits.

The World Cup two-man bobsled competition was held on December 9 and 10. Both the Tal/Devon and Sammy/Michael teams finished all four heats, and that was enough to meet the basic requirement for the Olympics in Calgary. In fact, the Jamaicans came in 32nd and 34th place, respectively, out of a total of 41 teams. The unexpected achievement of beating a number of national teams, even if well into the bottom half, garnered the Jamaicans brief nods of respect from a couple of seasoned bobsledders who previously thought they couldn't do it.

Under FIBT and Olympic rules, it was the drivers who qualified, not the pushers, which allowed the drivers to make the final selection of who would be in the sled on race day. That rule meant that the pushers might not know if they would be racing a bobsled until just before competition—a perfect set-up to create discontent and quash expectations. At the time, nobody was concerned with how selection would shake out down the road.

The qualification and beating of other teams thrilled Devon, Michael, and Sammy. Ever the brooder, Tal was merely satisfied. He recognized they had barely mastered the basics and still faced a steep learning curve in an ever-shorter time frame. Tal knew they were still way behind when compared to all the other bobsledders going to the Olympics, even if they had good start times. The risk of failure loomed over him, as did the prospect of more crashes and more injuries.

Shortly after the race, the FIBT officials threw a wrench into what should have been a settled matter. They announced that the two Jamaican bobsled teams did not qualify for the Olympics after all. The FIBT contended that the Jamaicans needed to compete in the 1986 World Cup circuit race as well as one in 1987 to qualify. George had already researched the rules well before the team entered the World Cup and was not about to accept the FIBT judgment.

Furious, George and Will notified Mike Fennel, the president of the Jamaica Olympic Association, who involved Tony Bridge, Jamaica's representative at the IOC. Prince Albert also learned about the injustice and spoke with his own high-level contacts at the IOC and FIBT. The prince argued forcefully that the Jamaicans had met all the requirements. He pointedly told FIBT officials that they could not exclude the Jamaicans "just because *you* think they are a bunch of clowns."

A few days later, thanks to Bridge's and Prince Albert's behind-the-scenes objections, the matter quietly went away. Jamaica was going to the

Olympics. Still, some of the FIBT top brass deemed the Jamaicans unworthy of being bobsled Olympians, even if they relented and let them go. Detractors moved to the shadows, waiting.

CHAPTER 15

THROW IN A FOUR-MAN SLED TOO?

After qualifying for the Olympics in Austria, Tal, Michael, Devon, Sammy, and Freddie headed back home for Christmas. Upon arrival, they didn't get a reception or much of a reaction. The sport was still foreign, and people didn't understand why Jamaica was even going to the Winter Olympics. Jamaica's leading newspaper, *The Daily Gleaner*, where Pastor Dudley was now the editor, printed one article about the team. The sports writer labeled the whole enterprise a "party for rich boys." The Spartan living conditions during training in Calgary and Igls had been anything but a party, but that didn't seem to register. Tal's family was generally supportive, even if they knew virtually nothing about bobsledding and found the initiative a bit strange.

On New Year's Day, the team flew to New York's JFK Airport. Pat picked them up and drove them to Saranac Lake, outside Lake Placid, where they stayed at his mom's house for the night. The next day, Pat took them to the Lake Placid bobsled course that they were unable to slide on three months earlier. This time, the track was iced and ready to use, and the two-man sled they had "acquired" in Austria had arrived.

With the Olympics just six weeks away, the team felt the pressure to cram in all the training they could. The Jamaicans had shown they could make it down a track most of the time. But this was the Olympics, and they were still neophytes in a rough-and-tumble contest filled with testosterone-fueled and sometimes violent athletes. Acceptance into the exclusive, clubby circle of jacked-up competitive bobsledders addicted to the adrenaline rush of high speed and bragging rights seemed beyond reach.

Lake Placid hosted the 1932 and 1980 Winter Olympics and had been the venue for several World Championships. All the American and Canadian bobsledders, as well as other sledders from other countries, had trained on the Mt. Van Hoevenberg track since it was, until Calgary, the only bobsled course in the Western Hemisphere. The initial natural track built for the 1932 Olympics was carved out of forested wilderness in 1930. The German engineer who designed the track took a radically different approach to the European runs, making it steeper, longer, and far more precarious. At the very first international competition held on the track in 1930, a Belgian bobsledder was killed. For decades after that, the Mt. Van Hoevenberg track was stuck with the reputation of being the most difficult and dangerous track in the world. Everyone who went down it knew they stood a much higher risk of crashing and getting injured or even being killed.

When the IOC awarded the 1980 Winter Olympics to Lake Placid, the local bobsled community persuaded city and state officials to build a modern artificial track in accordance with international standards. The track was still steeper, with tighter curves than other modern tracks. At the track's first international competition before the 1980 Olympics, several bobsledders crashed and some suffered serious injuries. The reputation of the track in Lake Placid as being the most intimidating track in the world remained intact, forcing even the most seasoned of sledders to pump themselves up before going down.

For the Jamaicans, training on the notorious track in Lake Placid battered them far more than the tracks in Calgary and Igls, so much so that the guys needed more recovery time. To keep the training schedule going with rotations, Devon suggested to George that he bring onboard Caswell Allen to train with them. Caswell, who was living in nearby Toronto, had already been selected as an alternate during the tryouts in September and pushed the sled contraption on wheels on a few occasions in Jamaica. But he had still never touched a real bobsled. Nonetheless, he was "an athlete in waiting." George approved, even though Caswell had a lot of catching up to do. Unlike Tal, Devon, Michael, and Sammy, however, Caswell didn't share the same enthusiasm for bobsledding they had, especially after a particularly bone-rattling run. Still, he practiced with the team.

Around the second week in January, Sammy suddenly turned melancholy. Despite being on the cusp of entering the Olympics with a guaranteed spot as a driver, he announced he was quitting the team. Tal postulates that Sammy's mounting personal problems had simply overwhelmed him to the point where he just couldn't go on. The nature of those problems has never been disclosed, but they were severe enough for him to walk away. Regardless of the cause, Sammy was no longer part of the team and left Lake Placid. He never spoke with Tal again or, apparently, any of the other team members.

Sammy's departure left Tal as the only driver on the team. Nobody else could steer a sled, which meant Jamaica had only one two-man sled to enter with Tal plus one pusher/brakeman. Devon was the clear favorite since he had raced in the Igls qualifying event with Tal. Michael became the first alternate, with Caswell as the second. Freddie had pretty much bowed out, even though he was still on the roster.

Sometime during training at Lake Placid, George, without discussing it with anyone, brazenly contacted the IOC about allowing Jamaica to enter a four-man sled along with the two-man sled. The Jamaicans had not raced or qualified in a four-man sled and had never even gone down a track in one. But the concept had a certain appeal because it played to Jamaica's strength in pushing. Four strong pushers would, in theory, give them a faster start compared to some other teams, and that could translate into a faster finish. It would also give more sledders a chance to race in the Olympics instead of just Tal and Devon. George asked Tal how he felt about driving the four-man sled as well as the two-man, assuming that the FIBT would allow it. He said he would be willing to give it a go.

The nature of the conversations between George and the IOC has been lost to time. As a good-old-boys network in 1988, the FIBT had a lot of flexibility in making decisions. However, the fact that Jamaica had not entered a World Cup race in the four-man event should have closed the option. Perhaps the FIBT did not want another fight with George over eligibility, as they had over the qualification of the Jamaican two-man sled a month earlier. Or George may have reminded the FIBT that the Jamaican team was generating positive public interest in the sport that, until then, had been relatively obscure compared to the glam sports of Alpine skiing and figure skating.

Somehow, George's powers of persuasion convinced someone high up in the FIBT command to give the green light and let the Jamaicans quietly slip into the Calgary Olympics with a four-man sled. George almost certainly did not mention to the FIBT board that none of the Jamaicans had ever been in a four-man sled. And the FIBT likely assumed they had been practicing in a four-man sled to be ready; otherwise, they would not be asking for the exemption. After all, who would even consider entering a four-man bobsled, with the Olympics only a few weeks away, if they had never been in one? Once again, a door that looked tightly shut had opened, driven by George's unwavering insistence.

In Lake Placid, Pat found an old four-man sled that the team could borrow and might even be able to buy. Unlike the two-man sleds, the heavier four-man ones require more coordination on the push and loading. They go faster and are harder to control. Tal noticed right away the difference in steering but got the feel for it after three good practice runs, even on Lake Placid's tough and unforgiving track.

On the fourth run, Tal hit the wall and badly wrecked the sled, even as he continued down the track. George paid to get it fixed, but nobody wanted to use the beaten-up sled for the race. He and the team figured they would take their chances and acquire another one after arriving in Calgary. At least they got some practice time in the four-man sled, even if just for four minutes. Although George had hustled to get Jamaica's four-man team approved for the Olympics, both he and Will worried privately that the guys might not be ready. The last thing on anyone's mind was the lurking scourge of violent Jamaican drug gangs a few miles away.

CHAPTER 16

"HANDS UP!"

I n the 1970s and 80s, Jamaican drug gangs, often linked to a political party, expanded well beyond their strongholds in the poor Kingston neighborhoods of Trench Town and Tivoli Gardens. They staked out turf in the big cities of New York, Philadelphia, Washington, D.C., and Toronto, often pushing into the territories of longtime US organized crime gangs with ruthless violence. Their total disregard for life approach, honed in the toughest Kingston streets, enabled the gangs to corner much of the market for marijuana and later, crack cocaine. They called themselves "Posses," a lame attempt to sound like or imitate cowboy posses of the Wild West. One of the gangs later took the name "Shower," which referred either to a political party in Jamaica showering them with money or to the gangs showering opponents with bullets or both. Sometimes gangs went by the name "Yardie," which was normally a term of endearment Jamaicans called each other, as when friends gather to enjoy backyard BBQ parties. Outside Jamaica, the term somehow became twisted to refer to a Jamaican drug gang.

Unlike previous gangs that simply imported the drugs and sold them to another gang for distribution, the Jamaican gangs brought in drugs and took over the direct-to-consumer market. This vertical consolidation of the business gave them astronomically higher profit margins. At the time, they could buy one kilo of cocaine from a Colombian cartel for $5000, which could earn them $120,000 in street sales. As the gangs became more powerful and better organized, they diversified into illegal arms sales and money laundering. The promise of quick riches allowed the gangs to recruit thousands of members and set up networks in more cities. Hundreds of homicides followed.

By the mid-1980s, the gangs had moved into rural America, including upstate New York. The surge of drugs, plus the complete disregard for human life, severely burdened local police departments that had to deal with a whole new level of international crime. In 1987, police in Albany and Saranac Lake made a bust, thanks to an undercover agent who managed to infiltrate the gang. That resulted in a handful of arrests. In retaliation, the gang members who had not been apprehended brazenly called for attacks on local law enforcement. Knowing how viciously the gangs operated, the threats put local police departments on high alert.

* * *

As the Jamaican bobsledders finished up their training in Lake Placid at the end of January, news media stories about them going to the Olympics spilled out. The incongruity of a bobsled team from the tropics was tailor-made for an easy, attention-grabbing laugh. Almost no one in the press took them seriously and treated the entire effort as whimsy. One exception was *People* magazine. The editors found out about the team training in Lake Placid and sent 1976 gold medal Olympic decathlete Bruce Jenner (now Caitlyn Jenner) to Jamaica to interview the team. World-class athlete Jenner recognized the athletic commitment the Jamaican bobsledders had made to the sport and wrote one of the few accurate articles about the team. Nobody associated with the Jamaican team had reached out to the press, but they got publicity anyhow.

When the Jamaican Consulate in New York City learned that the Jamaican bobsled team was preparing for the Olympics in upstate New York, they insisted that the team stop in before flying back to Kingston so they could host a reception in their honor. The consulate and the New York City Jamaican community, at least, took them seriously.

Just before leaving Lake Placid, the team had the two-man sled painted in the black, green, and gold colors of the Jamaican flag so it looked sharp and ready for the Olympics. On their last night, Pat took the team to a popular bar nearby for beers. For a while, the pressure was off, and Tal, Devon, Michael, Caswell and Freddie could finally relax. They all proudly wore their Jamaican Bobsled Team jackets to the bar, and the patrons—all white—immediately recognized who they were and were aware of their training at the nearby Lake Placid bobsled run.

Everyone wanted to meet them and buy them a round, so the drinks flowed freely. The unaccustomed attention helped make the physical and mental thrashing they had taken every day on the course more bearable. At around two in the morning, Pat and the Jamaicans left the bar and stepped out into the chilly air and quiet street with nobody around. Suddenly, two police squad cars with lights flashing darted out of a side street straight at them. Police officers in flak jackets armed with rifles jumped out and ordered the men to put their hands up. Tal felt the cold barrel of one of the rifles press against his neck. Pat, the white guy in the group, shouted to the police that the black guys were members of the Jamaican bobsled team and training in Lake Placid. He pulled out a badge showing he had worked for a local security company and told the cops he knew the Saranac Lake police chief.

The police backed off and started asking questions about what they were doing there. After 10 minutes, the police became convinced that these five black guys really were Jamaican athletes and not the Jamaican drug gangsters they were looking for. The cops returned to their squad cars and drove off, leaving the team, once again, alone on the cold and empty street.

The Jamaicans, of course, were well aware of incidents of police brutality and racism in the US, though they themselves seldom, if ever, faced racial discrimination. Certainly not in Jamaica. The police now targeting them was a realization of what could happen to American black men walking the street late at night in a white area. But the police stop with guns drawn was also a curiosity. They knew they were innocent and quite confident that whatever misunderstanding with the police would be cleared up quickly.

Indeed, three of the Jamaican bobsledders were soldiers in the JDF and had worked with Jamaican law enforcement at one time or another in their military capacity. But they had never had the experience of being confronted by police on mere suspicion because they were black and Jamaican. They did not fully understand the consequences of a random stop like this or sense the same gut-wrenching worry that a black American man would feel in the same situation.

The guys joked among themselves about the strange and unexpected encounter and speculated about what led the police to detain them just outside the bar minutes after they had left. They quickly concluded that one of the ladies in the bar who had taken a special interest in them must have upset the man she was with. Possibly aware that Jamaican drug gangs were operating in the area, the jealous boyfriend likely found a devious way to retaliate. He knew he would lose any bar fight with five very fit athletes, so that option was out. But he could make a quick phone call, tipping off the police to a bunch of "suspicious" Jamaicans hanging out at the bar, and then hope the police would swoop down on them once they left.

If that is what the resentful boyfriend thought would happen, he got it right. Never mind that Tal, Devon, Michael, Caswell, and Freddie were innocent bobsledders. But just the fact that they were Jamaicans in a town with police on high alert over violent threats was enough to trigger a SWAT team operation on very short notice.

Once more, a case of police profiling of black males in America had reared its ugly head. While law enforcement sensitivity to the real danger posed by Jamaican drug gangs was certainly understandable, a single tip from a guy about some Jamaicans drinking beer in a bar hardly warrants an armed bust on the streets. One could ask if a group of Irish athletes drinking in a bar where Irish gangs happen to operate would be subjected to the same ambush. And why didn't the local police question the tipper further to validate who these Jamaicans in the bar were? For example, what were they wearing? Jamaican bobsled jackets would hardly be the garb of choice for drug gang members.

In this case, the rush to judgment with nothing more than a tip about some black Jamaicans in a bar speaks to how law enforcement can be misapplied. A concerned citizen alerting police about a perceived suspicion is a common occurrence. So is the police response by probing the veracity of the call before taking action, especially one that is not an emergency. But not in this case. The absence of effort to ascertain what was really going on apparently enabled a jilted or wanna-be boyfriend to stick it to Jamaicans for being a little too popular with at least one woman.

One can only imagine how the otherwise innocuous enjoyment of a few bottles of beer in a bar could have turned into tragedy. It only takes a single agitated cop who can't keep his nerves in check to flick off the safety and pull the trigger because he figures that Jamaicans are all violent drug dealers. None of the Jamaican bobsledders, in fact, held it against the police or any American. They appreciated what the Americans had done to take them to the Olympics. At the same time, they got more than a glimpse of what police overreach in America looked like. And now, they too could speak from experience as they headed to New York City for the first of many receptions on their way to Olympic history.

PART THREE:

HERE WE ARE/ HERE WE IS

CHAPTER 17

CAN THIS BE HAPPENING?

Back in Jamaica, the reaction to fielding a bobsled team at the Winter Olympics continued to be tepid. On one level, the few Jamaicans that cared didn't expect their team to be among the contenders, as they were new to an unknown sport. On another level, the long tradition of Jamaican Olympic excellence created assumptions that they would not disappoint. At least Prime Minister Edward Seaga appreciated what they were doing, in large part. because the positive media attention distracted from the negative coverage of gang violence.

The team put on a confident air. Tal, like the others, shook hands and gave smiling acknowledgements. On the inside, he knew full well the demands of going up against highly experienced bobsledders who looked down on new and inexperienced interlopers. Tal didn't just want to make it down the bobsled chute four times without crashing. He wanted to beat a few nations along the way. He wasn't in it to enjoy the pageantry of the Olympics or just to call himself an Olympian.

George and Will formally announced the team selection: Tal as captain and driver of the two-man sled and Devon, Michael, Caswell, and Freddie as eligible pushers/brakemen. Privately, George also brought up with Jamaican sports authorities his discussions with the FIBT and the possible addition of a four-man bobsled, a new prospective challenge that ratcheted up expectations of the still-green team. At this point, momentum had built, and there was no turning back.

Tal had the final say on who would be the brakeman/pusher racing with him. Since Devon had always been the second man with Tal in training and competition, the assumption was that he would keep that position in Calgary. The others would be alternates and march in the opening ceremonies, as well as live in the Olympic Village with the other athletes. But they wouldn't compete unless the Jamaicans could actually secure a four-man sled to use, and the FIBT didn't change its mind about letting them compete.

Along with the bobsledders, the Jamaican Bobsleigh Federation designated Will to march in the opening ceremonies as national representative. George would march as *Chef de Mission* (Head of Delegation), while P.C. Harris would join as delegate. The team selected Tal to carry the Jamaican flag.

Pat had traveled with the team from New York for his first trip to Jamaica and got a taste of the pride in the brand-new Winter Olympic athletes, even if confined to a small circle of people. When the Jamaican sports authorities brought out the uniforms the Jamaicans would wear in the opening ceremonies, Pat gasped. These were summer uniforms that consisted of smart-looking yellow jackets and black pants, the colors of the Jamaican flag, and a white shirt. Where was the coat to keep them warm in the cold? Pat called on a Calgary garment maker, Carrie Sprug, to get them proper coats and hats once they got there. Another Calgary garment company, Domini, set about making and donating proper Lycra race suits, which the team still did not have.

After a week in Jamaica, the team flew to Toronto for their first international fundraiser at a restaurant organized by a prominent Jamaican residing in the city. When they landed, they got another taste of celebrityhood. The Canadian immigration and customs officials congratulated the Jamaican athletes as they presented passports and collected their suitcases. As they exited the terminal into the blustery cold of a Canadian winter, more than one hundred fans welcomed them with banners, signs, and loud cheers. Big black limousines pulled up, the kind reserved for rock stars, and whisked them away to a fancy hotel in the city. The team rather enjoyed the unexpected VIP treatment.

Unfortunately, despite all the good intentions, the money raised at the restaurant venue barely covered the expense of bringing in the team. At least they received lots of encouragement and goodwill from the Toronto supporters, and it all felt good and real. The warm Toronto welcome foreshadowed the far greater frenzy to come the next day.

CHAPTER 18

CALGARY STAMPEDE

After flying into Calgary from Toronto, the Jamaican bobsledders slipped through the airport and caught a ride to the Olympic Village without much fuss. Once in the Olympic Village, however, the Olympic athletes quickly recognized the team and asked to be photographed with them. Even the big-name medal contenders wanted a picture hugging the Jamaicans.

Outside the Olympic Village, people went wild at the sight of the Jamaicans, who were easily identified by their "Jamaican Bobsled Team" jackets, to the point where they removed the jackets before going out. Even Denise, who had arrived and been invited to stay with a Canadian family, was pressed for autographs and was offered hundreds of dollars for her Jamaican bobsled jacket. The incongruity of black men from a tropical island participating in a winter sport at the Olympics resounded with excitement. "Hobbin' and a Bobbin'" became an instant hit that played everywhere and amplified the Jamaican presence. Soon enough, people learned the first few lines and sang along whenever they heard the tune.

The Olympic media could not get enough of the Jamaicans either and angled for interviews and photos. This was not limited to the paparazzi. Well-established outlets capitalized on the mania too and gladly fed it. A February 14, 1988, account in the *Los Angeles Times* reflects the media hype as well as the portrayal of the Jamaican bobsledders.

WINTER OLYMPICS: Notes: The Jamaicans Arrive Hobbin' and A Bobbin'

By Thomas Bonk

TIMES STAFF WRITER

Can a bobsled team from Jamaica find happiness and a medal in the Winter Olympics?

You've got to be kidding.

Jamaicans do not belong on bobsleds, they belong on the beach. At least that's the common perception, but all that is changing at the Winter Olympics, where the Caribbean country of Jamaica is fielding a bobsled team for the first time. No one gives the five-man Jamaican team much of a chance to be competitive, but the Jamaicans are already gold medalists in one race—the merchandising race.

Buried further down in the article are statements by George making several points about the team's challenges and aspirations. The article managed to squeeze out one quote by a single Jamaican bobsledder, Tal, who was asked to describe the feeling of bobsledding. He said, "Nice, man." Apparently, no more commentary was sought or needed from an actual Jamaican athlete who would soon race down the track.

All the mental and physical struggle to make it to the Olympics didn't matter. Nor did the fact that they sold T-shirts to pay for food and took on personal debt to be in Calgary. All that would have been a distraction to the far catchier and one-dimensional version of Caribbean black men who belonged on a tropical beach showing up in chilly Calgary with hilarious audacity that they could be winter sports athletes. Deprecating comparisons to comical British ski jumper "Eddy the Eagle," aka Edward Davis Edwards, abounded and hurt.

The glam factor continued at the bobsled hospitality tent, where all the bobsledders gathered with sponsors displaying their products from sleds to shoes. Normally, the press and guests would gravitate toward the favorites: Wolfgang Hoppe from East Germany, Switzerland's Gustav Weder, and Yanis Kipur representing the Soviet Union. But the crowd paid scant attention to them. Hanging out with the Jamaicans and getting that ultra-cool photo op counted more. The overwhelmed Jamaicans couldn't believe their surging popularity.

Only Tal grumbled. He knew they were not in the same league as athletes who had been training for years to be Olympic bobsledders and compete at this level at this moment. The Jamaicans were popular because they were unusual, not because of any demonstrated talent. That frustrated Tal more than anything, and he sensed how ephemeral that popularity could be once the novelty wore off. While the rest of the team regaled in the fun and attention and partied late into the night, Tal distanced himself. The team had not yet proven themselves other than to qualify by finishing four runs at the competition in Igls. Meanwhile, the doubters and detractors watched from afar at the circus-like attention on the upstart Jamaicans and waited for them to fail.

On the streets of Calgary, Freddie sold plenty of T-shirts, but not as many as he might have. The Jamaican presence had become so well known that hustlers were selling knockoffs of the Jamaican bobsled team image and keeping the proceeds for themselves. Financially benefiting from the Jamaican bobsled team had turned into a cottage industry that would grow exponentially. While upsetting, the team and team managers were too preoccupied to institute legal proceedings to stop it.

The Olympic opening ceremonies commenced on February 13, with Tal leading the Jamaican delegation. For him, holding the Jamaican flag was one of the proudest moments of his life. Devon, Michael, Caswell, Freddie, Will, George, and P.C. Harris followed, along with the rest of the delegation, all waving to the crowd and thrilled to be there. The crowd roared as they marched by. Indeed, the whole world by then had become caught up in the phenomena of the black men from the tropical Caribbean competing at the lily-white Winter Olympics. Jamaican IOC members Michael Fennel and Keith Shervington anxiously wanted everyone marching to be perfect ambassadors while representing Jamaica at its first Winter Olympics. Only George was out of place, as he had chosen to wear a souvenir cowboy hat given to athletes by the Calgary Olympic Committee instead of the cap issued by the Jamaican Bobsled Federation.

The Jamaican bobsled team was not the only entry from the Caribbean or a non-winter sport country. Puerto Rico, the US Virgin Islands, and the Netherlands Antilles had all entered bobsled teams, as had teams from Taiwan, Mexico, Portugal, and Monaco. None of them received anything close to the attention and adulation accorded to the Jamaicans.

The opening ceremony itself highlighted Western Canadian culture with recognition of First Nation tribes and more than 300 two-stepping country-western dancers. The only glitch came when, shortly before the opening ceremony, the organizers learned that the 62,000 specially made ponchos could not be distributed to the attendees. IOC officials discovered that the ponchos had a Coca-Cola logo, but the soda company was not an official Olympic sponsor. The organizers hastily sent the ponchos to local jails to have prisoners turn the ponchos inside out and remove the unsanctioned logos. The prisoners did the work, but some of them decided to "stick it to the man" and slipped in profanities on the ponchos, which forced organizers to sort through all 62,000 and discard the offensive ones.

The Jamaicans had shipped the two-man sled acquired in Lake Placid. But they still needed a four-man sled to actually compete in what had become a highly anticipated event. Somehow, the press had not picked up on the fact that the Jamaicans were still sled-less two weeks before the four-man race. Luckily, Pat located an old four-man sled parked in the refrigeration house under the track and notified George that it was for sale. The Canadian owner asked for $25,000. George countered with $5000, but the owner wouldn't budge. So, George grudgingly forked over the full price.

George had extended himself once again, even quietly drawing on the joint bank account with his wife Patricia. But he had had enough of carrying all the financing on his shoulders. George wanted the team to get out and raise more money to contribute to the mounting expenses he was covering, the sled being the latest. That's when he took it upon himself to capitalize on the team's publicity and organize a party. He contacted a popular Calgary bar and nightclub called *Orestes* about hosting the fundraising event and charging for admission. George got an enthusiastic "OK," even with the short notice.

Word about the party with Jamaican bobsledders spread quickly. The next night, a long line snaking around the block formed outside *Orestes*. Inside the packed bar, Tal, Devon, Michael, Caswell, and Freddie got up and sang a rendition of "Hobbin' and a Bobbin'" to wild cheers. Freddie grabbed his guitar and followed up by singing one of his favorites, the very melancholy and mournful song, "A Whiter Shade of Pale," by Procol Harum. It fell flat with the audience, who were clearly in a hopping mood. Sensing the letdown, Freddie quickly pivoted and played the far livelier and more appropriate Bob Marley song, "Stir It Up," which brought down the house. The cash from the admission and T-shirts raised just enough to pay George back for the sled.

CHAPTER 19

A KICK IN THE GUT

The two-man bobsled competition was set to take place on the weekend of February 20 and 21, a week after the opening ceremony. That would give all competitors two practice runs a day down the track over the next five days. At least Tal and the team had some experience on the course, and they would be sliding in their familiar two-man sled that had been shipped out to Calgary from Lake Placid.

When the Olympic bobsledders were not doing practice runs, they usually worked on improving their pushes and loading skills at a separate push track over a flat surface next to the bobsled course. A modified bobsled on wheels running over rails simulated the critical first 15 meters from the starting blocks plus a 50-meter start zone without having to slide down the course. Tal, Devon, and Michael had the push down pretty well. They had already practiced hard on the wheeled sled contraption at the JDF base in Kingston a long five months earlier, in addition to training runs in Igls, Lake Placid, and Calgary. Caswell had made practice pushes too, but he didn't have nearly the experience of Devon and Michael.

The Olympics followed the same procedures as World Cup events. Each team would race two heats on the first day (Saturday) and two heats the next (Sunday). The order would be determined by a random drawing of all the entries. The aggregate times of all four heats would determine the team standings and who stood on the podium with medals. Combining times always made it possible for a team to move up in the standings on later runs if any of the front-runners faltered. Thus, a bobsled team with consistently good times in all four heats could win, even if they did not post the fastest time in any of the heats. At the same time, a team that had two or three first-place heats could stumble in the last heat and be out of medal contention. Any crash where the sledders did not complete the course would result in a DNF for "Did Not Finish."

The Jamaicans weren't racing for a medal, of course, but they wanted respectable results. If things went their way, they might come in the middle of the pack of 41 teams entered in the two-man event. That might at least shut up the lingering naysayers at FIBT and other doubters, including much of the media, who still considered the Jamaicans more comedians than athletes. Tal, especially, had not come this far in preparing and qualifying for the Olympics just for the thrill of being in the Calgary Games.

From time to time, Howard stopped by to check on the team. Even though he was now an official juror for the bobsled competition and charged with overseeing fairness, he quite improperly took time to point out what they could be doing better. The team, and Tal in particular, greatly appreciated Howard's presence and the fine-tuning advice he gave on the side, even if his "coaching" bent, if not broke, the rules. They welcomed all the help they could get.

Halfway through the week before the two-man race, Howard watched Devon and Michael alternate pushing and loading the sled with Tal. Neither Freddie nor Caswell were being considered for the two-man team. Howard noticed that Michael looked to be the faster of the two. But Devon had always been the brakeman and pusher with Tal during training and in competition at Igls and assumed he would be the one to race. Howard suggested to Tal that he should make two runs down the track, first with Michael and then with Devon, for a final determination of who should be the pusher/brakeman on the two-man team. The winner would be the one who clocked the best push time over the start zone on the racecourse. A race-off to finalize the team was not unusual. Only the driver was officially entered on the team initially, which allowed for last-minute changes to the pushers.

In the first run down the track, Michael posted his fastest time ever through the start zone—faster than Devon had in past pushes. Tal told Howard that when Michael pushed, it felt like he "took the bob right out of my hands," meaning the pressure Tal had on the front bar dissipated as Michael accelerated. That was all Howard needed to hear. Despite being an Olympic juror for bobsledding and not supposed to be advising on the selection of a final team member, Howard essentially made the call that Michael be the pusher/brakeman in place of Devon. Tal and George agreed.

Howard, Tal, and George were so convinced that Michael was the superior pusher that they didn't give Devon his own run to see if he could push faster. Minds had been made up. For Devon, losing that chance at this stage was, as he put it, "like a kick in the gut." He was beyond upset. Devon blamed Tal for making the last-minute switch to Michael without giving him a chance, a reproach that would strain the relationship between them for the next decade. Now, all Devon could do was watch.

*　*　*

A day before the two-man bobsled event was to begin, Tal's brother, Chris, flew to Calgary from Spokane, Washington, to watch Tal race. He wasn't planning on attending because he had a big track race coming up the following week, but Tal had called and urged Chris to come to Calgary, a short flight north. Chris had already begun his second semester of an MBA program at Washington State University in the Pullman School of Business, where he was also training for the 1988 Summer Olympics as a sprinter. The year before, he had graduated from the University of Idaho, where he ran track and was rated as one of the 10 best sprinters in the world.

Chris looked forward to cheering on Tal and the Jamaican team. He had already watched Tal carry the flag in the opening ceremonies on TV from his dorm room and felt a surge of pride for both his brother and their home country. Pat picked up Chris at the airport and arranged for him to stay with local Canadian hosts.

Like most brothers with a couple of years of age difference, Chris and Tal had similarities and quite opposite temperaments. Both grew into adulthood exceptionally intelligent and academic, thanks mostly to Blossom and Pastor Dudley's emphasis on education and insistence on obedience. Each would find their callings that fit their personalities. Tal took to military discipline and flying helicopters that demanded methodical precision, total concentration, and mechanical savvy. Chris, on the other hand, enjoyed interacting with large groups and would later find his niche as an investment banker, providing sound advice to wealthy clients. The rivalry would always be there, but they always stood by each other, particularly when a crisis hit. As much as anyone, Chris understood the pressures Tal was facing to perform in the Olympics after being introduced to the sport only five months earlier. He wanted to see Tal and the team be the best they could, not knowing that his own life was about to take a profound turn.

CHAPTER 20

MOTHER NATURE MAKES AN APPEARANCE

On Saturday, the first day of the two-man bobsled competition, a blast of warm air blew into Calgary. Called "Chinook," these storms roar in from the Pacific Ocean and push up against the western slope of the Rocky Mountains. By the time the clouds reach the 12,000-foot summits, all the moisture has been wrung out. The remaining dry air rolls down the eastern slope of the mountain range and sweeps across the Alberta prairie, picking up dust and sand as it heats up.

The natural phenomena shows up a dozen or so times during the winter, causing dramatic temperature swings. During the Olympics, the temperature in Calgary went from 10°F to 64°F (−12°C to 18°C) in one day, a huge 54°F (30°C) swing that made the city almost as balmy as Miami. The name of the warm wind is derived from the Chinook First Nation, or American Indian people native to the Pacific Northwest. In their language, they call the wind "snow eater" because of the way the warm wind consumes or vaporizes the snow.

Chinook winds are normally welcome breaks from the bone-chilling cold of winter. But not during the Olympics, as they wreaked havoc with the schedules of just about every outdoor sport dependent on snow. The refrigeration generators cooling the coils under the bobsled track barely kept the temperature at the required −11°C. What officials could not control, however, was a layer of dust and sand settling on the track's ice coating.

On race day, for the first two heats of the two-man bobsled, all the sledders wondered how the warm weather and the first signs of dust and sand would affect the performance. Tal began his preparation ritual by walking the track to study each turn once more. He closed his eyes to visualize exactly how he would make the turns while feeling the force of gravity push against his back and butt up to 5 Gs. As Tal had learned, sensing the sled was as important as seeing the track and making slight adjustments with the ropes to guide the sled over the optimal line for maximum speed.

After completing his walk-through, Tal joined with Michael and Pat to put their sled in the truck and drive it to the top of the hill. They lined up the sled along with the others in the order of their turn to go and waited for officials who stopped by to check it for compliance. The officials first asked the team to remove the scabbards or rail covers so they could press a sensor on the side of each runner to take the temperature. Then they checked the temperature against a reference runner that established the outside temperature to verify that it did not vary more than 4°C. Officials also checked the sleds for mechanical compliance to ensure there were no technological tweaks or add-ons in violation of FIBT rules. This period could be nerve-wracking for sledders, who often pushed the rules to the limit or beyond to gain a small but crucial advantage.

Below the start house, Prince Albert of Monaco approached Tal and told him that Denise had wished him "good luck."

"Oh, Dudley!" the prince said in a lighthearted manner. "Please tell your wife that she can't wish anyone good luck. Saying 'good luck' actually brings us bad luck!" Ironically, Prince Albert's Team Monaco had drawn lucky number 1 in the start order that would ensure them the smoothest, fastest ice. Bobsledders are not normally a superstitious lot, but Prince Albert clearly did not want to jinx the good luck that had already come his way.

All teams passed inspection and were cleared to race. Howard walked about the start house and watched as Tal and Michael pushed the sled onto the start blocks but said nothing. Tal felt the intensity and pressure of the moment—the circus of cameras and crowds milling about, as well as the expectations of his first Olympic run. At this stage, however, he had already begun judging himself against the clock and the track and less against competitors. He went into the Olympic Games internalizing the competition against himself.

When the buzzer sounded, Tal and Michael got off to a good start with a solid push through the fly and start zone. Tal navigated each turn close to how he had seen them in his mind but still posted a disappointing time of 60.20 seconds that would put them in 34th place. The defending World Champion and heavy favorite, Wolfgang Hoppe from East Germany (German Democratic Republic, or GDR), followed later in the heat and piloted his sled to the fastest time at 57.06 seconds.

In the second heat, sand and dust from the Chinook continued to settle on the track. Tal and Michael were among the early starters when the ice was still decent, even if showing signs of deterioration. The worsening ice conditions slowed down their times slightly, but not as much if they had started later when the track became even slower. That was good enough to put them in 22nd place overall—right in the middle of the pack. At the end of the run, Tal went over to Howard and told him he was physically and mentally exhausted. Instead of an encouraging pep talk, Howard barked at Tal to get his head back in the right place and focus on the competition.

By the time many of the faster bobsledders had their turn to slide later in the second heat, more sand and dust had fallen on the ice, causing a more noticeable friction against the sled rails. Times significantly slowed. Hoppe, who was one of the last to race, dropped from 1st to 8th place by clocking a disheartening time for him of 59.26 seconds. He complained bitterly to officials about the track conditions, comparing it to "running on sandpaper." When no action was taken, he and other top sledders filed a protest, demanding that the results from the first two heats be disallowed. Officials denied the protest. Hoppe also blasted inexperienced bobsledders for messing up the track with their erratic driving, though none by name.

For the third heat on Sunday, conditions went from bad to worse. Again, Tal and Michael started early in the heat and posted an even slower time, which was expected given the deteriorating track conditions. However, their aggregated times over three heats boosted them to 16th place and into the upper half of the contenders. Unfortunately, that did not last long. After 28 out of the 41 sleds had gone in the third heat, officials decided to postpone the remainder of the heat and all of the fourth heat until the next day on Monday.

When the two-man competition resumed, the track was not completely cleared of sand but far better than the previous day. The sledders who had not completed their third heats the day before went down the track in considerably faster conditions. The postponement benefited Hoppe in particular, who posted the fastest times in the last two heats of the day. But it was not enough to make up for the lost time due to the sand on the second heat. He had to settle for silver, while the Soviet team of Yanis Kipurs and Vladimir Koslov won gold.

The cancellation of part of the third heat and resumption on Monday badly hurt Tal and Michael. They posted a time of 61.23 seconds in the fourth and final heat. That knocked them down to 30th final place out of 41 when the times were aggregated—not bad considering how new they were to bobsledding. Still, the race mentally drained Tal, as he had not yet developed the sustained focus required for Olympic-level competition.

The decision to reschedule part of the third heat and all of the fourth until the next day, of course, begs the question of what is fair. Did officials make the right call because the speed of the ice had changed over the duration of the race due to natural conditions? By comparison, in ski racing, the fastest racers in the first run are slotted to go in reverse order during the second and final run. But they don't get a postponement because a warming sun has turned the snow slushy toward the end of the race. Had half of the third bobsled heat and all of the fourth heat not been canceled on Sunday, the Jamaicans might very well have remained in 16th place or close to it. Indeed, those who came after the Jamaicans all posted slower times than in previous heats.

At least George had fulfilled his promise to Jamaican Olympic Association President Michael Fennel about beating ten or more teams in the Olympics, despite the ruling that deprived the Jamaicans of an even higher standing. In fact, they beat 11 teams, showing that Jamaicans could compete on the world stage against other newbies, even though they had less training.

The Olympics have long had their political moments but far fewer in the Winter Olympics and never by bobsledders. That changed when Kipurs, who was a Latvian, painted his two-man sled in the red and white stripes of the Latvian flag to protest the Soviet occupation of his Baltic country. His gold medal run in that sled, broadcast around the world, gave the protest a higher profile and made the victory even sweeter.

Three years later, in 1991, the Soviet Union collapsed, and Latvia became free again. From then on, Kipurs and other Latvian bobsledders would represent their own country. They remained world-class challengers, even against Russia, in part because the only Soviet Union bobsled track at the time was located in Latvia.

East Germany would collapse and fold into West Germany even sooner when the Berlin Wall came down in October 1989, 21 months after the Winter Games. All the East German athletes after that competed under one Republic of Germany flag that enhanced an already powerful German bobsled machine. Meanwhile, the Jamaicans were about to make their own indelible mark on world sports history, though not the one they wanted.

CHAPTER 21

LAST-MINUTE MAN

The four-man bobsled event was set for the weekend of February 27 and 28, with 26 teams entered. Over the next four days, each team would again get two practice runs per day on the course before racing in the first two heats on Saturday. The final two heats on Sunday would come a few hours before the closing ceremony that evening.

On Monday afternoon, right after the completion of the delayed two-man race, Tal, Devon, Michael, and Caswell began preparing for the four-man event. George had the newly acquired sled painted over with the green, black, and yellow colors of the Jamaican flag, just like the two-man sled. The sled hardly measured up to the latest tech standards of the other sleds, but at least it looked good. The team inspected the sled for flaws and gave it a tune-up. The runners in particular needed to be smoothed with fine sandpaper and aligned properly with the steering mechanism to ensure maximum speed. It would never be anything close to what the top competitors had, but it would have to do.

Although Tal beat 11 teams in the two-man event, the four-man sled was a different animal—more cumbersome, less forgiving, and faster. With only four practice runs piloting the sled in Lake Placid, including a bad smack against the wall on the last, he had reason to worry, even as he stifled his doubts.

At the push-track practice area, the team went through the start routine by hitting the push bars at the same time, sprinting as fast as they could, and loading in the right sequence. Chris stopped by to watch, as did

Howard. Tal introduced Chris to Howard, noting that Chris was one of the best sprinters in the world. Howard already knew that, as did everyone else, and asked Tal why Chris wasn't on the team with that kind of speed. Tal told him that they were considering Chris for next year.

During one of the practice pushes, Caswell slipped and fell off, hurting his hand. It is not quite clear how bad the injury was, but Caswell either could not race or did not want to race. Freddie wasn't considered an alternate to take Caswell's place since he had already established his comfort level as the entertaining member of the Jamaican bobsled team who loved the limelight—not the risk-taking sledder going down the chute 85 miles an hour.

With only three guys left, racing in the four-man event now depended entirely on getting one more sledder to push. All eyes looked at Tal's brother. George was also well aware of Chris's athletic excellence, which led to suspicions that George and Tal had wanted Chris to be on the team all along. And it was no secret that George didn't like Caswell because he didn't see him as fit or dependable enough. The exact circumstances of Caswell's departure remain muddled. Caswell's injury may or may not have been a convenient way for him to exit without fanfare, especially since he never shared the same enthusiasm as Tal, Devon, and Michael. Either way, his exit paved the way for Chris to take his place, even though no decision had been made. Caswell did not protest, and everybody played it cool.

Tal asked Chris to come push with the team on Tuesday, which Chris did without expectations since he had never touched a bobsled until then, but Tal and the others pointed out the basics of pushing and hopping in. Tal and George wanted to see how Chris performed, with an audacious intent to recruit him on the spot if he took to the sport. Remarkably, no one was particularly worried about actually being able to race the four-man sled in the competition just days away. A constant state of flux in the Jamaican camp had become the norm. Somehow it would come together, as it always did at the last minute. In the meantime, Will obtained credentials for Chris to stay in the Olympic Village with the team, while George worked on certifying him as a Jamaican Olympian with the IOC. Back then, looser rules meant people in positions of authority had more leeway to make things happen.

Chris had a steep learning curve. While struggling a bit with the push and loading technique, he showed exceptional speed on the push-track, as one might expect of a top Jamaican sprinter. On Wednesday, the team positioned their sled for their first practice run down the track and had Chris sit in the sled while they pushed. Having one of the team members sit in the sled at the start instead of pushing was not a good image in front of other bobsledders, as it screamed "inexperienced." Chris didn't have to do anything but sit still, tuck in tightly, and feel the speed and gravitational forces on his body as the sled shot down the track. Unfortunately, Chris made the rookie mistake of not wearing padding on his arms, even though he was advised to do so. At the end of the run, he had badly bruised his elbows from all the banging in the sled.

Back at the push-track, Chris had trouble with the load timing as a side pusher. Devon, who had been the brakeman, switched places with Chris to make him the brakeman. Entering directly from the open back of the sled as the last man was easier than jumping in from the side. On Thursday's practice run, Chris finally demonstrated that he could push the sled as the brakeman and jump in last without a problem.

The next day, Friday, one day before the race, Chris received official IOC approval to be on the Jamaican team. Again, George had persuaded some official to get his way. By now, his credentials as a swashbuckling hustler who never took no for an answer had been etched in stone. P.C. Harris suggested that George may have been a Caribbean pirate in a past life and never left that character behind. Pushy, tenacious, occasionally mad but never sad, George was born for this moment.

Once Caswell was off the team, Chris sensed that he might be asked to replace him, but that was only a possibility. As he put it in his own book, *Cool Runnings and Beyond: The Story of the Jamaican Bobsleigh Team*, "I was slowly and unconsciously merging into the team from Tuesday to Friday." Now it was real, and Chris, officially an Olympic athlete, would get one more practice run down the chute for a total of two before he pushed the four-man sled in his first race. Meanwhile, Tal's mental energy since the two-man race had returned and boosted his confidence, spilling at times into brashness.

CHAPTER 22

ALL EYES ON THE FOUR-MAN RACE

The week before the four-man bobsled event, the US hockey team played West Germany to decide who would be in the six-team medal round. ABC Sports, which held the Olympic broadcasting rights in 1988, covered the game and hoped for a US win, as that would keep a high number of American TV viewers watching the Games. Unfortunately for ABC, West Germany beat the US 4-1, knocking them out of the competition. Without the US hockey team playing, anxious ABC Sports executives looked for another sport to fill the Olympic airtime they had already paid for. The four-man bobsled event seemed like a good prospect, especially with all the hype around the Jamaicans. Instead of just showing highlights, ABC Sports decided to broadcast all four heats with John Morgan as the commentator.

John's rollicking, engaging observations in front of the mic reflected his deep roots in bobsledding. He had grown up in a big, tight-knit, well-known family of eleven siblings in Lake Placid. He, his father, and his brothers had all been bobsledders. John tried out for the US team for the 1980 Olympics, set to be held in his hometown that year, but didn't make it. Four years earlier, his oldest brother Jimmy, nicknamed "Nitro" for his explosive driving style, had made the team for the 1976 Winter Olympics in Innsbruck. Jimmy continued to race at the world-class level, while John moved on to a TV career, commentating on bobsled races.

Drawing on his knowledge of the sport that had been so much a part of his life, John proved to have a gift for making the races exciting. Mindful that the world tuned into Olympic bobsledding once every four years, he made a point of explaining the nuances of what was happening in the plain language of small-town America. Beginning in 1984, every American TV network that held the broadcast rights to the Olympics—ABC, CBS, and NBC—had hired John to provide the bobsled commentary. Over the years, John became the voice of bobsledding. Behind the scenes, he wrangled constantly with network executives, who wanted less explanation and more entertainment. For him, that approach was the surest road to sucking out the passion and flavor of bobsledding's TV coverage. But he was caught in a no-win ratings game that also called for longer commercial breaks. Sharing his insights and observations about bobsled racing with viewers had become deeply personal to John.

In 1981, three years before his Olympic broadcasting debut, ABC Sports hired John to help cover the World Championships in Cortina d'Ampezzo, Italy, with veteran sports commentator Bill Flemming. Cortina had been the site of the 1956 Winter Olympics and seven other bobsled World Championships. By coincidence, his brother Jimmy would be piloting one of the US four-man sleds in the competition. John was excited to be commenting live on a big race that included his brother taking on the world's best.

On the first day of competition, Jimmy's two heats had been slower than normal, putting him in 9th place. Disappointed, he was determined to make up for time on the third and fourth heats the next day. The team got off to a good start but was still running behind the leaders. Halfway down the course, John remarked on air, "His nickname is 'Nitro,' so I don't think he's going to hold back at all."

When Jimmy took the last curve before the stretch to the finish, he banked high and slammed into the guard rail, flipping the sled on its side. As the cameras rolled, John and Bill kept talking and hoping the sledders were okay. Soon, three bobbing heads could be seen slowly trying to squeeze out from under the sled while the medics rushed over. The driver in front did not move. Jimmy's head had hit the wall, pushing it back so the leather strap of his helmet cut deep into his throat. John's big brother, the one he looked up to, the sledder who had always made it down the track unscathed, died instantly on the ice.

* * *

John had observed the Jamaicans train and watched Tal and Michael race in the two-man event the week before. He had seen thousands of races in the US and abroad since he first began broadcasting bobsled competitions. John quickly knew the sledders who had it and those who didn't—the ones who just wanted the glamor because it provided an easier path to enter the Olympics than other winter sports. For these gate-crashers, he had no respect and didn't hold back what he thought. They were little more than wannabes in a sport that demanded athletic discipline, dedication, and courage.

The Jamaicans, however, were different. John called them true athletes. Early on, he realized they had the tenacity and talent to be better. "These bobsledders," he said, giving the ultimate compliment, "are the guys I want to be in the foxhole with." That assessment set him apart from broadcasters and reporters from other media outlets who saw the Jamaicans as an endless source of amusement. For all their commitment, however, John could also tell that Tal needed more practice driving a sled to compete at this level.

* * *

As the sun rose on the day of the first two heats, Tal, Devon, Michael, and Chris woke up early, packed their gear, and caught a bus to the track where Pat was waiting. Together, they readied the sled before loading it onto a van and driving it to the start at the top of the hill. Tal broke off from the team to begin his meditation ritual by walking over the track to study the curves. Once more, he closed his eyes and stitched together one turn after the other and saw himself sliding through each of them. Again, he anticipated the 5-G force pressure ramming down on his body as he entered the banks. Finally, he leaned down to touch the ice and imagined the runners of his sled gliding across, almost frictionless, at 85 miles an hour. In two hours, this track would be his entire world, with each run lasting under a minute.

The team loaded the sled onto the van and drove to the top of the hill. They carefully unloaded the sled and carried it upside down to the *fermé*, or closed area, where they placed it on a stand with the runners facing up. While waiting for race officials to make their final checks on the sleds, the Jamaicans took notice of the gathering bobsled royalty: Ekkehard Fasser and Gustav Weder from Switzerland, Ingo Appelt from Austria, along with East Germany's Wolfgang Hoppe, and the Soviet Union's Janis Kipurs lining up with their sleds. An entourage of managers, mechanics, and coaches swirled around them. The Jamaicans had an entourage of one, Pat, who had his hands full keeping things moving on schedule.

The inspection of the Jamaican sled, including the temperature of the runners, went off without a hitch. None of the other big-time bobsledders worried about the Jamaicans and their old sled breaking any rules, as they were hardly a threat to take a medal. The top sledders quietly focused on their well-known rivals.

The sleds were close enough so that each team could study the competition and try to detect the slightest mechanical enhancement, legal or illegal. The Jamaicans also watched the race preparations to see what the best sledders did to fine-tune their equipment. Just about every experienced bobsledder believed that somebody, if not everybody, was cheating or trying to cheat, and they openly talked about it. Rumors about one team or another gaining an unfair advantage spread quickly in the small bobsled community. The usually unverified stories served to "explain" why one team did better than expected, even if the evidence was sparse.

Years later, US bobsled assistant coach and former Olympian Mike Kohn captured the scuttlebutt best: "The problem is that we're only on the track for 57 seconds. The rest of the time, we're sitting around speculating and coming up with conspiracy theories about what people are doing." Top Canadian bobsled pilot Lyndon Rush said it more bluntly, if not entirely accurately: "{Cheating} is part of our sport. If you ain't cheating, you ain't racing." He added, "If you're doping, that's not forgivable. And it's not always cheating. It's interpretation of the rules. You don't call it cheating."

The most brazen bobsled rumor circulating at the Calgary Olympics alleged that the Soviets had developed a clever way to heat their runners without being detected. Supposedly, they had inserted a heating fluid into the fiber glass fittings that were placed over the runners, leaving the bottom exposed. The purpose of the fittings was to provide better aerodynamic flow as the sled descended down the course. However, the Soviets would attach the fittings after race officials had measured the temperature of the runners and certified them as being within the allotted 4°C variance. Once the team flipped the sled over with the runners flat against the ice, the fluid would be activated by gravity and seep along the edge of the runners to warm them up just enough to have an advantage. Nobody could prove anything, but the suspicion persisted, and the next year, the FIBT banned the use of the fittings.

In the random drawing for starting position, the Jamaicans lucked out and drew an early number that would give them faster ice. At least they did not have to contend with sand and dust on the track this time.

CHAPTER 23

"WE'RE BETTER THAN THIS"

Tal didn't like to believe that he also harbored superstitions, but having Coach Howard around seemed to calm him and give him confidence. As he and his teammates moved the sled against the start blocks, Howard's reassuring presence was there, even if nothing was said between them. George, too, gave Tal a nod, as if to say, "You got this." Tal let his mind relax and focused on the present. Again, he rehearsed in his mind the turns he would take, feeling the pressure points and finding the line.

When the 60-second buzzer sounded, the team methodically wrapped their fingers around the push bar handles. Devon called the words "Ready, Set, Go!" and the team sprinted as fast as they could. But in the middle of the 50-meter start zone, as they were gaining good momentum, Tal's push bar broke, causing him to fall on his side. Still, he managed to twist his way into the sled with striking agility, but the mishap lost critical time. The team finished with a disappointing time of 58.04 seconds, which put them third from the bottom, barely ahead of Portugal and Australia. In addition to falling after the bar broke, Tal had hit the retaining walls too many times on the straightaways, which slowed their time further. At least he zipped through the 360° Kreisel turn without mishap. As in the two-man sled, East Germany's Hoppe took the lead, clocking in at 56.16 seconds.

On the second run, the Jamaicans got off to another poor start. This time, Michael had leaped in at the right time but stood erect for a couple of seconds, unable to sit down properly between Devon and Chris. Though he finally tucked in with the others, the loading looked inept and cut into their speed. They finished with an even slower time of 59.37 seconds, which put them just second from the bottom in front of Portugal after aggregating times. Kipurs piloted the Soviet team to the best time in the second heat at 57.28 seconds. But Hoppe from East Germany still had a solid lead after the first day and was the clear favorite to win the gold.

The disappointing Jamaican performance was exacerbated by the feeling that they should have beaten other new teams such as New Zealand, Romania, Australia, Chinese Taipei, and Bulgaria. At least the Jamaicans had a chance to better their standing in the final two heats the next day.

That evening, back at the Olympic Village, Tal checked out a VHS tape of the race that Olympic officials had produced and brought it back to the room to play for the team. In particular, he wanted to review the atrocious loading of the sled that they were supposed to have under control. After watching and noting the errors, Tal asked everyone in the room to leave except for Devon. As the number two man in the sled who sat just behind Tal, Devon had a tendency to look over Tal's shoulder instead of tucking his head down. Tal didn't mince words when he told Devon that he was driving the sled, not Devon, and to cut it out because it was throwing off his focus. Devon didn't say anything and glared before walking away.

The next morning, Tal put his hand against his forehead and felt the heat. His nose was clogged, his throat was sore, and his head was so stuffed up that he felt it might burst. Every part of him ached, and he knew he had caught the flu that was going around the Olympic Village. His body screamed for him to stay in bed, but he shook it off, just as he had done with all disappointments. Still groggy, Tal struggled to put on his Lycra race suit before grabbing his gear pack and catching a ride to the track. In the meantime, Devon, Michael, and Chris met with Pat and loaded the sled in the truck to get it ready at the top.

Alone, Tal trekked up the iced chute to picture in his mind, once more, the turns he would negotiate in an hour. The steps felt heavier as he fought the nausea and tried to break through the fog in his head. At turn four near the top of the course, where the track steepens sharply, Tal slipped backwards, smacking his shoulder hard on the ice. The pain from what turned out to be a broken collar bone radiated deep into the bone. But Tal got back up, continued walking to the top, and refocused on the race and the moment. He was good at that—in high school, at Sandhurst, flying helicopters. Tal could compartmentalize and shut things out that did not matter, but today it was much harder.

At the top, Tal met up with the team and waited for bobsled officials to check out the sled for illegal alterations and take the temperatures of the runners. After officials certified the sled as compliant, the Jamaicans moved closer to the start. They would be among the early sliders that morning. All the while, Tal mentally reviewed the course in his head as he stayed in the present. When the last team in front of them cleared the track at the bottom, officials signaled for the Jamaicans to move their sled against the start blocks.

With all of his senses tuned, Tal peered down the gleaming track that reflected back the bright sunlight. Fans in the stands rattled their cowbells for Jamaica, now everyone's favorite team. Even Denise had been given a cow bell to ring as she stood near the start house with other guests with special passes. For Tal, it was no longer about just making it down and being satisfied with that. He wanted to excel—to get it right this time. Entering deeper into a transcendent state, Tal attempted to quell each grim affliction one by one. Tal didn't believe in demons, but they came for him anyhow, testing and jeering and meaner than ever.

Tal stifled the pain in his shoulder and the drag on his body from the flu. He put aside the falling-out with Devon after favoring Michael in the two-man sled, as well as Devon's annoying habit of pressing his goggles into the nape of his neck to get a look at the track as the sled hurled down the chute. Tal let go of the expectations built up about the underdog fairy-tale team from the tropical island that everyone in Calgary, Jamaica, and around the world wanted to behold. With exactly nine runs in a four-man bobsled, doubts resurfaced about being a real bobsledder. But he choked off those thoughts too.

Tal craned his neck to scan the scene for Howard, the bobsled champ who believed in them. Tal needed a believer on his side today, even if Howard had given him a hard time in the two-man race. But Howard was nowhere to be found. George sensed Tal's distraction and made a fateful decision to tell him that Howard was flying back to New York that morning. That hit Tal hard. One more demon to taunt him.

When the buzzer sounded for the start of the 60-second window to begin the push, Tal pulled down his goggles, which triggered a laser focus and doused the fears. The adrenaline rush kicked in. Each man grabbed the push bar tightly, heads looking down at the ice, their brains on autopilot to go all-out. The team rocked the sled back and forth from the starting block as Devon called out, "Ready Set, Go!" They sprinted faster over the start zone than ever before, 5.35 seconds, the seventh fastest of the race, and loaded perfectly into the sled. They had a chance.

CHAPTER 24

THE CRASH

The sled quickly gained speed as it descended the track and zoomed through the first curve a little high on the bank. With each subsequent curve, John Morgan saw that Tal's steering had slipped farther and farther behind. "They don't have the experience! They don't have the experience!" he shouted anxiously into the mic. By the time the Jamaicans reached the treacherous Kreisel turn, almost halfway down the course, Tal had missed too many pressure points. The sled traveled too far up the bank and began "porpoising," or bouncing up and down, as Tal lost control. The sled flipped over on its side, smashing into the retaining wall at 85 miles per hour (136 km/h).

As the pilot, Tal took the brunt of the impact, his head hitting hard against the ice, and it kept hitting again and again as the sled continued sliding down with nothing to stop it. His life flashed before his eyes, where he vividly saw Denise, their kids, Blossom, Pastor Dudley, Terry, and Chris, who was sitting in the back of the sled. He despaired, thinking of the grief his mother would feel if both her sons were killed in the crash.

John's worries about Tal's driving suddenly became real. He barked in the mic as if the Jamaicans could hear him: "Stay in the sled, stay in the sled!"

After ten seconds, Tal's brain snapped into survival mode. He went through the crash drill of trying to protect his head by tucking it under the lip of the cowl in front of him. But the protruding "snout" of the motorcycle helmet he was using prevented him from tucking lower, which also made it harder for his teammates behind him to get their heads out of the way.

The Jamaicans careened down the track with the sled on its side, and their skulls slammed against the wall for another 18 seconds. In what seemed like a crash that would never end, a calm came over Tal.

"There was nothing I could do except watch the ice go by as the sled slid toward the finish line. In that moment of strange relaxation, it occurred to me that what we were doing was not correct. That there's a right way to do it, and here was not the end. I went through in my mind what was needed to become top-class in bobsledding. We would need to raise money, market the product, get decent equipment, get more coaching, travel, and time on the ice."

Chris, with only two training runs in any kind of sled, had never crashed. He felt the impact and saw the ice sliding by out of the corner of his eye. He also smelled the burning of plastic from his helmet skidding against the ice but was not sure what to do, as there had been no time to train him in crash procedures. He rode it out, tucking himself as tight as he could into the hull.

Denise and Pat watched in horror on the TV screen at the top of the course. Pat called for Denise to get in the truck with him and rushed to the bottom. George, too, saw the crash on the TV screen. His heart sank as he shoved his way through the crowd toward the finish line, thinking they might all be dead. George blamed himself and wondered how he would tell their mothers.

When the sled finally stopped, time stood still as everyone looked for movements among the men still tucked into the hull of the sled. Slowly, each sledder from the battered team climbed out, dazed, and detached. Their brains still on autopilot, they righted the sled and pushed it the rest of the way to the finish line. They did not carry it as portrayed in *Cool*

Runnings. Dramatizing the crash further would have made no sense and did not even occur to them. Plus, the sled was too heavy for such a stunt.

Spectators applauded politely but not uproariously. Tal, Devon, Michael, and Chris, surprised, waved back, but this was not a moment to relish. Their debut in the four-man sled was over and recorded as a DNF (Did Not Finish), the only one of the 26 entries in the race. At this darkest hour, Tal chided himself for not having enough training. He would never again race a bobsled unprepared.

Back in Jamaica, Blossom and Terry, Tal and Chris's little sister, were outside tending to the garden when the telephone rang. Pastor Dudley had called to comfort them, as he assumed that they had seen the race on TV, and let them know that Tal and Chris and the rest were okay.

The Swiss sled piloted by Fasser won the gold after upsetting the favorite Hoppe with an aggregate time of 3:47.51. Hoppe's disappointing third run evaporated his lead, knocking him into second place for the silver. Kipurs took the bronze for the Soviets. The American sled piloted by Brent Rushlaw finished fourth, just missing the bronze and the podium by 2/100ths of a second, continuing the American medal drought since 1956.

But Jamaica's dramatic crash stood out in the public's mind as one of the defining moments of the Calgary Olympics. The unlikely team the world had come to love did not expect this ending. The mishap took the spotlight off the bobsledders who actually won the medals. More painfully, the debacle vindicated the naysayers, who could now say they were proven right. After all the media hype, the Jamaicans didn't have what it took.

Paradoxically, had the Jamaicans simply finished all four runs without incident and placed near the bottom in the standings, they would have likely faded from the public imagination and been left as a footnote in Olympic history. Instead, the crash put an exclamation point on the journey that would catch the attention of the ultimate publicity machine:

Hollywood. Until then, the team had wounds to lick and decisions to make about what to do next. They had hit rock bottom.

Tal took the loss the hardest. At the closing ceremony in Calgary, when the Olympic "Oslo" flag was handed over to the mayor of Albertville, France, the host for the next Olympics in 1992, Tal didn't feel like celebrating. He didn't even like being there. The agony of the crash gave him not just clarity but infused him with the will to keep going. In that deep ravine of humbling failure, Tal brashly believed that one day he, too, would slide among the elites of the sport.

CHAPTER 25

THE HARDER THEY COME

Tal, Devon, Michael, and Chris wondered how people back in Jamaica would take their spectacular failure. This was, after all, a country that usually brought home medals from the Olympics, not a DNF (Did Not Finish). With expectations dramatically dashed, they worried they might be the object of ridicule for not measuring up. When the bobsledders arrived home at the Kingston airport, a large crowd showed up, including the Minister of Tourism, and warmly greeted them with cheers, much to the team's surprise. That evening, the team was formally feted at the Devon House, an elegant 19th-century mansion. Prime Minister Edward Seaga, who hardly ever attended functions, came to this one to show his support.

Tal appreciated the welcome, even though he felt he did not deserve it. Still, it was good to know Jamaicans saw beyond failure and hailed the attempt. But he was hurting too much, physically as well as mentally, to fully enjoy the heartfelt support. His perfectionist nature did not allow for much joy when he fell short of achievement, particularly since responsibility for the crash fell squarely on him. Breaking his collar bone and bashing his head on the ice would take a while to heal. As painful as these ailments were, the disappointment at not performing better hurt more. Tal needed to turn his attention away from bobsledding for a while to gain a fresh perspective.

Chris, who gained instant fame by stepping into the sled at the last minute to replace Caswell, also anticipated a lukewarm reception back in Jamaica. He too found the unexpected, genuine support by his countrymen encouraging, if a bit odd, in view of the excruciating ending. Chris later reflected on his experiences in his book about Jamaica's bobsled team. He wrote in his book: "Much later, I came to understand what Jamaican bobsleigh meant to the people at this time and continues to mean. It's the finest part of the Olympic Movement. When I speak now about Jamaica bobsleigh, I speak about the Jamaica bobsleigh movement, which is an idea. It's not time on the ice. It's an idea that regardless of where you're from or your circumstances or who your parents were, you can move yourself into other places, you can make more of yourself. You can do more than you thought, more than people around you expect."

Devon also delighted in the warm welcome and noted his experiences in his book *Keep On Pushing: Hot Lessons from Cool Runnings*. "In my wildest imagination, I never thought that I would ever be called an Olympic legend. So thank you for that . . . Calgary was and still is a very special experience. It was a crazy endeavor, but it's been life-changing in so many ways, not just because I went to the Olympics and a movie was made. I think it's virtually impossible to take on a feat like that, and it doesn't cause you to grow as a person. So I'm grateful for that experience."

In Calgary, Tal had observed Chris using one of the first computers and determined that he would learn to type properly so he could use one too. He found an old typewriter and practiced every day. When he wasn't typing, he took time to restore an old travel trunk that his parents had used while traveling to and from the Turks and Caicos. The family heirloom he had taken after getting married had itself become beaten up with age and neglect and badly needed refurbishment to its original condition. These were good distractions for the next few weeks and helped him refocus on home and family, as well as his future in the JDF.

The question for those still in the bobsled game—Tal, Devon, Chris, Michael, Will, and George—was "Where do we go from here?" Six months earlier, against all odds, they all turned a fantasy into a reality. But impressive as their success was in reaching the Olympics, the crash high-lighted just how far they had to go to be competitive.

For all the personality conflicts and resentments right up to the last calamitous run, nobody wanted this journey to end at the bottom. They refused to be remembered as also-rans who received a lot of attention for being funny and different before flaming out. They knew now that it would take a lot more than just being good sprinters to play with the big boys.

*   *   *

A few months after returning to Jamaica, the Sagebrush Cantina just outside Los Angeles invited the team to make publicity appearances at the restaurant as well as at other venues. The team gladly accepted the all-expenses-paid trip to California, happy to finally reap some benefit from all their efforts. One of the nice perks included a stretch limo to drive everyone around.

At the time, Leo was studying for an MBA at the University of Southern California on a Fulbright scholarship. He had watched the team crash and, for an agonizing moment, thought they had all been killed. Tal reached out to Leo and asked him to join the group for the party at the Sagebrush Cantina. But Leo, now a financially strapped student, had no car or money to get to the cafe. So Tal asked the driver of the limo to take a detour to pick up a very surprised Leo at his student apartment. The lively get-together would lay the seeds for Leo to take on the management of the Jamaican bobsledding team down the road.

While in Los Angeles, Jerry Buss, one of the owners of the L.A. Lakers, asked the Jamaicans to be his guests at the upcoming game against the Houston Rockets. The team could only stay for half the game before heading off to another appearance. As the Jamaicans were about to leave the sports complex, they saw a huge hulking man whom they recognized as heavyweight boxing champion Mike Tyson. They talked among themselves about approaching him for autographs. Chris made the first move and started to walk up to Tyson but was interrupted by actor Lou Gossett, who got to Tyson first. After Gossett finished chatting and left, the whole team went up to Tyson and introduced themselves as being from the Jamaican bobsled team. While shaking their hands and smiling, Tyson said, "So what do you know, n****rs on ice, the n****rs on ice." The conversation did not deepen, as Chris recalled, but everyone got autographs.

* * *

In October 1988, Hurricane Gilbert, a Category 5 storm, made a direct hit on Jamaica, triggering mudslides and killing people. As soon as the hurricane passed, Tal opened the doors to one of the JDF hangars, rolled out his helicopter, and lifted off to assess the damage. He flew over the Blue Mountains, the most heavily hit part, and saw before him a white forest of trees with the bark stripped off by the force of the wind. He located the washed-out roads and villages in ruins and reported back to direct the rescue efforts. Being first on this disaster scene was the peak of his military career. After that, he would be back to the police work of finding ganja fields, a far cry from the mission of an army helicopter pilot that he had signed up for. That's when he decided to end his JDF career.

In 1989, Tal went into business with Will to establish Heli-Tours, a private helicopter charter company based in Kingston. They focused on tourists coming off cruise ships as well as executives and politicians who liked to project power and prestige by arriving in a private helicopter. He enjoyed the work and was glad that it would let him bobsled, assuming funding and support would continue.

* * *

An executive from Miller Lite contacted George about doing a TV commercial featuring someone from the Jamaican bobsled team as part of a series of commercials using "former" athletes as pitchmen. Apparently, the executives at Miller Lite assumed the Jamaicans were now ex-athletes after their debacle in Calgary. At least the Miller Lite people understood the world-wide popularity the Jamaicans had acquired through their short bob-sled adventure and wanted to capitalize on it while still hot. Miller Lite was ready to shoot the commercial in a week on a beach in Miami. They just needed one person to represent the team.

Freddie was the obvious choice, as he had always been the team enter-tainer and had the charisma to shine on camera. George and Freddie worked out a deal where Freddie would get 20% of the proceeds from Miller Lite and the Jamaican Bobsleigh Federation would get 80%. A commercial like this from a major American brewer paying big bucks was exactly the financial shot in the arm the team needed since they had nothing but debt.

George and Freddie caught a plane to Miami, where Miller Lite people met them at the airport and took them to the beach for filming. When they arrived, crews had set up the cameras and props and were ready to shoot. One minute before Freddie was about to step in front of the cameras, he pulled George aside and said, "I want 80%."

Shocked, George reminded him they had a deal for a 20-80 split, but Freddie said, "No!" He insisted on 80% and added, "If not, I'm walking."

Livid at the sudden switch, George lashed out, "What about the team?"

Freddie shrugged and said he had kids in school to support.

"Where, Switzerland?" George groused back.

Freddie likely thought this might be his last chance to benefit from the publicity of the Jamaican bobsled team and recoup the money he lost by not working for months. In any case, Freddie wasn't budging or bluffing, and the cameras were ready to roll. George decided to go with Freddie's revised terms, figuring 20% was better than nothing, and the federation needed money. But it was another low point that sapped enthusiasm for the future of Jamaican bobsledding just as they were on the cusp of creating a brand and raising enough money for the next Winter Olympics in the French Alps.

Tal Stokes with his mother Blossom O'Meally-Nelson Stokes
1963 in Grand Turk, Turks & Caicos Islands.

Courtesy Stokes Family

Siblings Chris, Terry and Tal Stokes in Jamaica circa 1969.

Courtesy Stokes Family

Tal Stokes, new recruit for officer training in the Jamaica Defense Force 1980.

Courtesy Blossom O'Mealley-Nelson

Denise Muir (Stokes) upon completion of officer basic training with the Jamaica Defense Force in 1981, the first woman to be fully integrated into JDF.

Tal Stokes at officer training Royal Military Academy Sandhurst 1981.

Tal Stokes with cousin Janine at Royal Military Academy,
Sandhurst graduation party 1983.

Courtesy Stokes Family

Denise Muir (Stokes) competing at body building competition circa 1985.

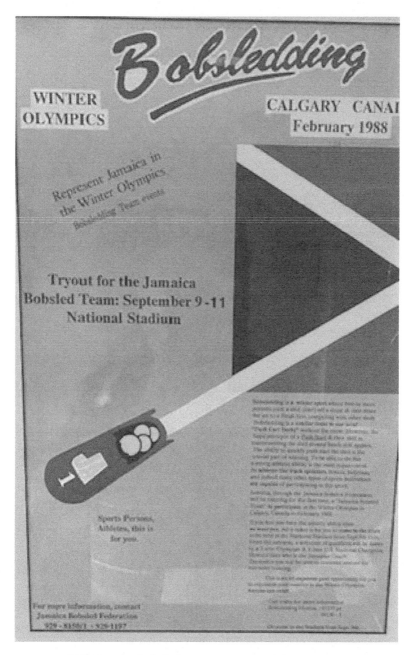

1987 Jamaica bobsled team tryout recruitment poster.

Tom Maloney, William Maloney, Nick Hanauer, Tal Stokes hanging out circa 1991.

Courtesy William Maloney

Tal Stokes using his own push training method in Jamaica
with son in the cart in 1993.

Courtesy Denise Stokes

Team manager Leo Campbell in Jamaica with team in
background practicing pushes in 1993.

Courtesy Leo Campbell

Chris and Tal Stokes in Chicago circa 1990.

Courtesy Denise Stokes

Ricky Macintosh and Sam Bock with officials checking runner temperatures at 1994 Winter Olympics in Lillehammer.

Courtesy Leo Campbell

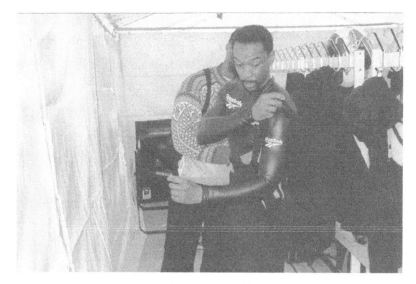

Tal Stokes suiting up for competition at the 1994 Winter Olympics in Lillehammer.

Stokes family at Legoland in Windsor, UK 2006.

Courtesy Stokes Family

Tal and Denise Stokes dressed up for date night circa 2008.

Courtesy Stokes Family

Jazmine Fenlator, Tal Stokes, Sepp Haidacher, Maria Haidacher, and Hannes
Conti at Haidacher home in Austria circa 2017.

Tal Stokes reflecting 2022.

Courtesy Denise Stokes

CHAPTER 26

THE ROAD TO ALBERTVILLE OLYMPICS '92

We had to change the culture or rather look at the culture that was successful in the sport, and which is typically a German culture. We had to go into German mode to get things done.

—Tal Stokes

Things would never again be normal for anyone associated with the 1988 Jamaican Olympic bobsled team. That quest had changed their lives forever. Wherever they went from then on, even decades later, that's what they would be remembered for. But no one knew that at the time. In fact, it seemed more likely the dream of becoming a bobsled nation might fade—a one-off anomaly, especially since they were all mired in debt and had no plan for what to do next. One thing was clear to Tal—if they were going to train for the Olympics in Albertville, they would do so as serious bobsled athletes, not as novelties.

Lack of money would be the biggest challenge, especially since both Will and George were practically tapped out. George, in particular, was miffed that he spent $90,000 without much likelihood of seeing any of it again. Still, Will and George committed themselves to what they had started, even if the future looked bleak. They met regularly with Tal and Chris to talk about the next steps and what they would cost. Prime Minister

Seaga stood firm in their corner. He had bought into the idea of building up Jamaica's image as a Winter Olympics contender. Moreover, Seaga fully appreciated the millions of dollars in publicity the Jamaican Olympic bobsled debut brought to the island, as well as diverting attention from the bad publicity over gangs and drugs.

Will had become close friends with the Prime Minister and was able to lay out for him what it would take to bring Jamaican bobsledding to the next level, including the monetary support required. Prime Minister Seaga didn't waste any time and directed the Tourist Board to amp up the funding. Will and George called on big Jamaican companies such as Red Stripe beer and Alcan, the bauxite mining and aluminum producer, to come on board as major sponsors. Enticing them to commit would take more time, but at least Appleton Rum was still on board. In the meantime, funding fell far short of what they needed to compete with the best.

Everyone sensed that Team Jamaica Bobsled had developed the beginnings of a "brand." Thanks to P.C. Harris's marketing imagination in Kingston and Calgary and the sheer audacity of the early visionaries, supporters, and bobsledders themselves for creating an Olympic team from scratch, people around the world immediately recognized "Jamaica Bobsled." George tried to obtain a US copyright for the name but was turned down because it was deemed to be in the public domain. More than anything, they needed to keep global awareness going to have any hope of generating money. And that meant increasing public media appearances by the bobsledders themselves.

Devon proved to be a natural at connecting with live audiences and on TV. Tal understood the publicity game too but had an aversion to the public relations aspect of being a celebrity, such as meeting and greeting, especially for TV show appearances. Others had to nudge and motivate him to smile and say something funny or interesting, even if it was just a one-liner. He had no interest in being a showman or being perceived as a glad-hander. He only wanted to be a competitive bobsledder and was ready to make the personal sacrifices.

In between branding engagements and strength-building workouts, Tal, Chris, Will, and George took time to lay out a simple, straightforward strategy for the next three years: train better, compete more, recruit strong athletes, and hire a good coach. Col. Ken Barnes continued to back the effort fully. Chris too had committed to staying with the team and put on hold his MBA studies and promising career as an education administrator at the University of Idaho. Chris also gave up on making the Jamaican Olympic track team as a sprinter—another difficult choice because he had a good chance of being selected. But he chose to focus on bobsledding, even though his father, Pastor Dudley, gave him flack for his decision.

It made sense for the team to build on the experience acquired by the four veterans of the crash while casting a wider net to attract new blood. At the time, only Ricky McIntosh demonstrated that he had the stuff to become another good bobsledder, and they brought him on the team.

The question naturally arose as to how to judiciously allocate the meager funding to ensure the most impact. Tal argued for concentrating the funds to train up just one two-man team along with one four-man team, as that would allow the best sledders the most ice time. He understood that world-class bobsledders spend just over two to two and a half hours on different tracks per season, way shorter than any other sport. Failure to meet even the minimal 120 minutes meant little to no chance of competing at the top level.

Others argued for using the scarce resources to develop more bobsledders for competition, even if that meant diluting the training time on the ice as well as competitive exposure. Both perspectives had merit, but the argument for funding more bobsledders and bobsleds prevailed to Tal's distress.

Meanwhile, the Jamaican bobsled team's popularity did not go unnoticed by the Soviet Union, which had a large trade mission in Jamaica. One of their trade representatives, George Bazanov, set up a meeting with Will, the president of the Jamaican Bobsled Federation, to discuss how the Soviets could support Jamaican bobsledding. Specifically, Bazanov proposed that the Jamaicans train on the bobsled track in Latvia, and the Soviet Union would pick up the expenses.

The irony of the Soviets contacting an American to link up with a Jamaican sports phenomenon certainly registered with all the players, as did the motivation for the initiative. The Cold War struggle between the Americans and the Soviets dominated and influenced all international relations, and almost no one thought it would end anytime soon. While practicing on the track in Latvia would have benefited the Jamaicans, Will, George, and Tal saw the invitation for what it was: a political propaganda effort to use the goodwill generated by Jamaican bobsledding to shore up the Soviet Union's poor image. They gave it no serious consideration. Bazarov persisted, but his government called him home after his tour of duty ended, and nothing more came of it. Two years later, the Soviet Union crumbled.

* * *

In the fall of 1988, the Jamaican team traveled back to the bobsled complex in Igls, Austria, to resume training and prepare to enter more World Cup events in preparation for Albertville. Upon arrival at the Landsportheim lodging, the director of the Igls track, Sepp Haidacher, introduced himself and welcomed them back. Over the decades, the burly and gregarious Sepp had become a legend in Austria and the wider bobsled world for promoting the sport. He had captained Austria's 1984 Olympic bobsled team in Sarajevo, even though he was not a bobsledder himself, and actively identified and nurtured promising young Austrian sledders, including future Olympic gold medalist Ingo Appelt, to be champions. His efforts would, in time, make Austria a powerhouse rival to the Swiss and Germans and eventually beat them.

Sepp had seen the Jamaicans learn bobsledding at Igls the first time they trained there in 1987 and observed them more closely at the Calgary Olympics. He, like TV commentator John Morgan, admired their commitment and spirit, despite the naysayers, and saw their potential to compete at a higher level. Although Sepp needed no more accolades, he essentially adopted the Jamaican team. He found them better equipment, helped them get better training, and, critically, taught them competition management. The Jamaicans could not have found a better friend in Sepp, who would ultimately be called their bobsled "Godfather." While not the official Jamaican coach, he advised and brought them closer to bobsledding's inner circle.

One of Sepp's first acts of assistance was to introduce the Jamaicans to a friend of his who built high-end bobsled trailers out of his garage in an alpine village near Igls. A week later, his friend produced a shiny trailer for the Jamaicans that looked like it could have come right off a Mercedes-Benz assembly line. A trailer doesn't seem like essential bobsled gear, but, in fact, all the serious European teams tow big trailers with sleds and gear from event to event across the continent. This proved to be a much more efficient way than shipping sleds in containers using freight forwarders. Not having to worry about whether their sled would arrive at the race venue on time allowed teams to focus more on the competition. For the Jamaicans, Sepp's generosity literally put them on the road to competing on a more level playing field that had eluded them when preparing for Calgary. Trailering sleds not only significantly eased the logistics burden but also highlighted the essential element of management to win.

* * *

The team faced its first big post-1988 Olympic international competition at the Cresta track in St. Moritz in early 1990. The natural track is more difficult compared to most of the artificial tracks because the curves lack precision engineering. Tal was having trouble getting through the sixth turn, known as the "Horseshoe," and crashed four times in a row while driving the two-man sled. Unlike almost all bobsled turns, the Horseshoe actually incorporated a slight upward slope before dipping steeply back down again, which Tal couldn't quite steer all the way through.

Switzerland's gold medal bobsledder, Gustav Weder, offered no sympathy and let Tal know where he stood by saying, "I've crashed four times in my entire career. Now you've just crashed four times on one curve." That stung, but Weder didn't say it out of malice. Rather, Weder's curt remark to Tal reflected his coldly analytical and academic approach to bobsledding using statistics. He studied each run and broke the segments down into units and knew, with a high degree of confidence, where he and every other top bobsledder would end up in the standings. Weder's unsubtle message to Tal: You have a long way to go in this sport. Earn it!

A far more engaging and friendly Swiss bobsledder, Nico Baracchi, recognized Tal's struggle with the turn and decided to help. He told Tal to close his eyes and hold out his hands. Nico took Tal's hands in his and gently guided them through steering the turn. Tal knew what he had to do after that and never crashed again on the Horseshoe turn or any turn on the Cresta run.

Over the next two years, Jamaican sledding skills steadily improved. But stretching limited resources to train Devon as a driver in the two-man sled while also improving Tal's capabilities hampered the advancement of both athletes. Neither received the hours of training needed to compete at the top level, as Tal had anticipated. In addition, the team had no formal coach. Sepp advised and, from time to time, would ask a local coach to observe the Jamaican training runs and give them feedback.

Notwithstanding limitations on training and competition and no full-time coach, Tal qualified for the 1992 Winter Olympics in both the two-man and four-man sleds, while Devon qualified in the two-man. Both earned enough points under the new FIBT rules for competing in four sanctioned races instead of just one, as had been the requirement in 1988.

As the Winter Games drew closer, Tal, Chris, Will, and George, still the de facto decision-makers for Jamaican bobsledding, concluded that they had to hire a coach to prep them properly as a competitive team. They didn't want to appear as amateurs winging it. One of Tal's British bobsled friends recommended fellow British bobsledder Peter Brugnani as the coach. Pete had raced for Great Britain in the 1984 Olympics in Sarajevo, so he had the experience and knowledge of what it took to compete at that level. He also happened to have a Ph.D. in mathematics, which gave him more analytical credibility, though it had limited application to bobsledding. All agreed to retain Brugnani in December 1991 as a coach through the Albertville Olympics.

Coach Pete carefully observed everyone's strengths and weaknesses in the short time remaining before the Olympic Games, just two months away. He noted, in particular, that Devon's driving had improved. At the pre-Olympic Igls training center in January 1992, he set up a race to decide who would drive Jamaica Team I and Jamaica Team II in the two-man race. Tal and Devon would race against each other twice with a different pusher. Tal won both races decisively, with even faster times than the US teams practicing, and was designated to lead Team I with Chris as his pusher/brakeman. Devon was paired with Ricky as his pusher/brakeman on Team II. Michael would be the alternate. Coach Pete would decide the four-man team later. Meanwhile, relations between Tal and Devon remained uneasy following the Calgary fallout over Tal's last-minute switch to Michael in the two-man. However, they kept it among themselves and out of the public eye, which fostered the image of a happy and unified Jamaican team.

The Jamaicans still needed good sleds if they were going to be competitive. Tal had his eye on the superfast "DDG" sleds from the former East Germany, sometimes called "DDR," with the initials for Deutsche Democratische Republik prominently painted on the front of the sled. (In English, DDR translates to "German Democratic Republic," though commonly referred to as East Germany.) Made by the Spezialtechnik bobsled factory in Dresden, these sleds regularly put the East Germans on the podium. Tal badly wanted one for Jamaica. The same Spezialtechnik factory also manufactured MiG fighter jets side by side with the bobsleds, even as late as 1991, two years after the fall of the Berlin Wall.

With the reunification of Germany, Spezialtechnik could no longer rely on government subsidies, as the company had under East Germany. One of the managers at Spezialtechnik, Karola Bräuer, sensed an opportunity and turned capitalist by setting up a company to sell the sleds internationally. Tal, dipping into his own entrepreneurial side, called Bräuer to propose a deal. Would she lease the DDG sleds to the Jamaicans for the Olympics and take "payment" in the form of publicity generated by being associated with the first Jamaican bobsled team? Bräuer agreed and let the Jamaicans borrow two two-man sleds and a four-man sled in Igls to take with them to the Olympics. After a couple of practice runs, the team loaded the sleds on the trailer provided by Sepp and drove directly to the La Plagne track near Albertville.

CHAPTER 27

DISAPPOINTMENT REIGNS

Upon arrival in the French Alps, the Jamaicans checked into the Club Med resort in La Plagne, which was being used as the Olympic Village for bobsledders only. The other Olympic athletes stayed in Albertville or near their competition venues scattered about. Lodging at separate locations isolated the athletes from each other and the public more than in previous Winter Olympics. The arrangement created a much different atmosphere compared to the local conviviality of Calgary, where the Jamaicans had been the main attraction. While still popular, Jamaica's endearing uniqueness in 1988 as tropical islanders competing in a Winter Olympic sport did not reach the intensity of Calgary. Some of the celebrity spotlight had shifted to the Mexican bobsledders, another incongruous phenomena similar to Jamaica. The Jamaicans were fine with being less in the public eye, even if they were still popular. They were in La Plagne to do a job—to prove themselves as real bobsledders, not look pretty for the cameras.

Devon carried the Jamaican flag in the opening ceremonies, followed by the rest of the team and delegation. Taking in the moment, they watched as dozens of acrobats performed a mesmerizing air ballet while suspended from poles radiating out from a tower high above the ground. The co-president of the 1992 Organizing Committee, Jean-Claude Killy, had been working for years to bring the Winter Games to Albertville and the Haute-Savoie alpine region of France. Since winning three Olympic gold medals in alpine skiing at the Winter Games in nearby Grenoble in 1968, he had plenty of clout and influence and spared no expense to make this one the grandest ever.

The Winter Games in Albertville featured 77 bobsledders competing from 25 nations, the largest number for an Olympic event, which would be the high-water mark. The increased participation was largely due to the still relative ease of entering a bobsled team, which also made plain the wide disparity between the pros and the inexperienced. That troubling trend would prompt the FIBT to impose even stricter qualifying rules with a quota to limit participation in future Olympics.

After good training runs in the two-man sled, both Tal and Devon were ready for the race set for the weekend of February 15 and 16. On Friday night, before the first two heats, Tal's bad luck struck again as he caught the Olympic flu once more. He woke up on Saturday groggy and aching all over but did not tell Coach Pete. Instead, he went about the business of walking the track to feel the ice conditions and mentally prepare for the race. He didn't slip this time, but he could barely see through the fog of sickness.

Tal performed poorly. Devon and Ricky beat Tal and Chris in all four heats, as they placed 35th and 36th, respectively, out of 46 teams. The aggregated times separated them by just over a second, at 4:11.68 vs. 4:12.76. Although both Jamaican teams placed in the bottom half, they still beat teams from Ireland, Bulgaria, Puerto Rico, Mexico, Monaco, and the US Virgin Islands. But beating those teams gave them little comfort.

Gustav Weder won gold for Switzerland together with Donat Acklin as pusher/brakeman. The now-unified German teams took silver and bronze with their two two-man teams, as expected. Ingo Appelt, driving for Austria's Team I, missed out on a medal by 4/100ths of a second. However, it was not a cakewalk for either Weder or the Germans, as Great Britain, Italy, and the second-string Austrian team were the front runners in the first day of heats. Fast times in the last two heats moved the medal winners just ahead of their rivals.

* * *

The US sledders finished below expectations in the two-man as well, garnering negative press coverage over team shakeups. The Americans had high hopes for getting back on the podium and possibly a shot at gold, especially since two-man sled driver Brian Shimer had just come off the 1992 World Cup with a bronze medal. A medal in these Olympic Games would have ended the American bobsled medal drought that had now increased to 36 years. But those hopes were dashed when Shimer's USA Team I came in 7th place, 69/100ths of a second behind Weder. That solid but discouraging result by Shimer and his pusher/brakeman, Minnesota Vikings star running back Herschel Walker, sparked an embarrassing controversy. The Washington Post suggested that Shimer blamed Walker's inexperience and clumsy entry into the sled for not winning a medal. Other press accounts have Shimer blaming not Walker but the failure to install the correct runners on the sled.

Regardless, a simmering squabble within the US team over competency began well before the Olympics. Since the mid-1980s, a few forward-leaning notables in the US bobsledding community have sought out professional American track and football stars to apply their athletic prowess as bobsled pushers. The US badly needed an edge to end European dominance of the sport. However, some of the cliquey upstate New York bobsledders who trained and hung out in Lake Placid felt uneasy about the newcomers. They grumbled that the pro-athletes hadn't put in the time to be competitive bobsled athletes. For the loose Lake Placid fraternity of sledders, the newbies had yet to master the precision agility required for a good start and synchronous movement while tucked into the sled. The Lake Placid sledders may also have had concerns about better athletes challenging them for Olympic team slots.

The American bobsled Olympic team selection process reflected the notion that experienced bobsledders who had developed a strong feel for pushing and descending down the track would produce the best results in competition. As a result, none of the pro-football or track athletes made the initial team for Albertville. The perceived lack of objectivity in picking who would represent the US prompted three pro-athletes—Greg Harrell, who played with the Los Angeles Raiders; Edwin Moses, a three-time Olympian with two golds and a bronze in the 400-meter hurdles; and Walker—to formally challenge the whole procedure.

One month prior to the Olympics, they petitioned a court to invalidate the push team selection, arguing that selection should be based on measurable abilities and not a subjective sense of what makes a good bobsledder. An arbitrator ruled in favor of the professional athletes and ordered a push-off competition to determine the final composition of the pushers on the teams. In January 1992, the push-off took place in a special push training facility in the former East Germany. Walker and Harrell won and joined the US team. (Moses dropped out to concentrate on training for the Summer Olympics.)

The judgment against the US bobsled establishment that required them to come up with an objective standard made sense. However, at the Olympics, Walker's push time over the 50-meter fly zone fell below par. No one questioned Walker's outstanding athletic ability, training ethic, or commitment as a team player. But his limited practice on the ice showed. In fact, Walker decided to switch over to bobsledding just ahead of the Olympics, largely because his team, the Minnesota Vikings, didn't make the NFL playoffs in the late fall of 1991.

Walker knew he had a problem. As early as the final pre-Olympic training in Igls, Walker admitted to Tal that he wasn't pushing fast enough. Tal chatted with Walker from time to time at the Club Med Resort in La Plagne and found him to be an easygoing, uncomplicated country fellow who happened to be a super athlete. Had Walker trained longer and learned to effectively transfer push power into sled speed, there is little doubt he would have been a far better bobsledder, given his exceptional athletic ability. In the two-man race, Walker may have taken some consolation in coming ahead of the USA's second team, piloted by Brian Richardson, with Harrell as pusher/brakeman.

* * *

The Jamaicans turned their attention to the four-man race set for the following weekend of February 21 and 22. In the very first four-man training run, however, Tal's legs got tangled in the steering ropes, which caused the sled to flip over midway through the course. There were no injuries, but a crane had to be called in to lift the sled off the course. The embarrassing moment, as spectators watched, harkened back to the 1988 crash and may have prompted second thoughts by Coach Pete about his confidence in Tal. But the coach didn't waiver in his support. Coach Pete also had to choose three pushers among the four remaining team members. He went with Chris, Mike, and Ricky, leaving Devon as the alternate.

Tal's flu had gone away, and he could once again focus properly. The team finished all four heats and placed 25th out of 31 teams. Although they continued to beat newbie teams like Chinese Taipei (Taiwan), Monaco, Mexico, and the US Virgin Islands, it still did not bring them pride. Officials disqualified the Canadian team after one of its pushers didn't make it onto the sled. At least nobody had anything negative to write about the Jamaican team for merely finishing well into the bottom half of the pack without crashing. The spotlight shifted back to the elite bobsled teams.

As in the two-man race, the Swiss and German bobsled superpowers were expected to sweep the medals in the four-man. But the Austrians, led by veteran pilot Ingo Appelt, slipped past them by just 2/100ths of a second for the gold. Germany's Wolfgang Hoppe, now driving for the unified German team, settled for silver, while Switzerland's Gustav Weder came in third for bronze. The gold almost went to Hoppe after Appelt struggled in the second heat with a troubling 10th-place finish. However, Appelt's excellent performances in the 1st, 3rd, and 4th runs made up the time and enabled the Austrians to walk away as winners.

In addition to being a formidable driver, Appelt had figured out how to make his runners glide fast over the ice. Coming from a prominent jeweler family in Austria, Appelt learned the techniques of cleaning and polishing fine jewelry for extra smoothness and applied them to the metal of the bobsled runners.

Germany Team II, driven by another former East German bob-sledder Harald Czudaj, had been favored for a medal. Shortly before the competition, however, he was accused of being an informant for Stasi, the East German security agency. Reports circulated that Stasi pressured him to spy on his fellow bobsledders in the 1980s in exchange for dropping a drunk driving charge against him. Olympic officials at first stopped Czudaj from competing, but he was cleared in time to drive the four-man sled for Germany Team II. The stress of dealing with the charges may have impacted his performance, as his sled finished in 6th place.

*   *   *

Meanwhile, the upheaval in the American team continued. Walker's performance in the two-man, as well as in subsequent training runs in the four-man, appeared to have influenced Randy Will, the pilot for the USA Team I four-man sled, to change out pushers. He replaced Walker with his Lake Placid friend, Chris Coleman, two days before the race. The US head coach, John Philbin, consented to the last-minute change, stating in the *Washington Post*, "Randy felt something was going on in the back of the sled that he wasn't comfortable with." Philbin added that the driver's "state of mind" was of utmost importance. The decision once more raised a question about the subjectivity of team selection criteria.

Walker took the decision to replace him on the four-man team in stride. He did not let it get him down, even if the call came down to sensitivity in the sled, as much as push speed. Tal could relate to the sometimes-difficult decisions. In Calgary, he was the one who decided to replace Devon with Michael in the two-man sled, a decision that had as much to do with what felt better as push performance. Three decades later, Walker would run for the US Senate in Georgia in one of the most contested and controversial senate races in modern US history.

Meanwhile, 3000 miles away from Albertville, NASCAR champion Geoff Bodine watched the Olympic bobsled competition unfold on TV in his North Carolina home. The US team shake-ups didn't concern him, but the sleds the Americans used did. He noticed that the Americans raced in European sleds, not American ones. When racing in Lake Placid, the Europeans usually sold their sleds to the Americans rather than ship them back home.

While plenty of people had tried to build a Made-in-America sled—even the giant car company GM gave it a go—all fizzled. That made the Americans dependent on acquiring sleds in Europe that were always at least a model year behind, as the top European teams kept the best for themselves. None of that sat right with Bodine. In fact, he found it downright unpatriotic. Upset and infused with a mission, he decided to bring the NASCAR approach to building fast race cars to developing fast bobsleds for American teams at the next Olympics and change the game.

* * *

The less than stellar Jamaican performance after four years of hard training precipitated another round of internal reflection on what they needed to do to be in the top 15, the elite level, and taken seriously. Driving back up the hill to the Club Med village after the last heat in the four-man race, a despondent Tal knew the team had the athleticism and that he had the steering ability. But when it came to bobsled managerial skills and ruthless focus, he made a troubling and piercing comment to his brother, "Maybe Black people can't do this."

PART FOUR:

HOLLYWOOD COMES KNOCKING

CHAPTER 28

THE COOL RUNNINGS LADY

I n late 1988, George connected with well known Hollywood director Michael Ritchie, who had directed *Down Hill Racer* starring Robert Redford, about doing a film featuring the Jamaican bobsled team. Intrigued, Ritchie bought the option to the story from George, Will, and the team for $20,000. He hired Lynn Siefert to write the script—a drama, not a comedy. The premise of the story centered on the rough and tumble streets of Kingston, which produced unlikely bobsled heroes. Siefert called the movie script *Blue Maaga*. Maaga means "skinny" in Jamaican slang, as in "malnourished." When used in conjunction with "Blue," however, the term maaga made no sense. Ritchie decided to go with the odd title anyhow and sold the script to Disney for $200,000 with a six-month option. George and P.C. Harris read the script and hated it, but they had no say over the story.

Enter Dawn Steel. In early 1991, Dawn was unceremoniously ousted from her job as president of Columbia Pictures when Sony bought the company. She had been the first woman to head a major Hollywood studio after having had a string of successes as head of production at Paramount Pictures. These included *When Harry Met Sally, Flashdance, Fatal Attraction*, and *Top Gun*, among others. Getting dumped from Columbia was a hard blow for Dawn, but she had dealt with setbacks before. She started her own one-woman production company, which had almost no chance of putting her back in the game at the same top level. Thanks to Dawn's connections with Disney CEO Michael Eisner and Chairman Jeffrey Katzenberg, old pals from her days at Paramount, she secured a contract as a producer. Her first task: go through a stack of scripts and see if any had potential.

Dawn's improbable journey to Hollywood started with humble beginnings in a struggling lower middle-class family in Long Island, NY. Both sets of her grandparents were Russian Jewish immigrants who barely escaped the pogroms in Ukraine around World War I. They brought with them deep sorrow, a no-frills work ethic, and an instinct for survival that was passed down to her hard-working parents. Her father, Nat Spielberg, was a competitive bodybuilder and called himself the "Man of Steel." He even went so far as to go by the name Nat Steel in his New York City athletic circles and Nat Spielberg for family and work, thus effectively living a double life depending on who he was with. When Dawn was born, he and Dawn's mother, Lillian, had to decide what last name to give her and chose "Steel."

Dawn was bright, but with lackluster grades and a family that struggled to pay monthly bills, she faced limited opportunities. When Dawn ran out of money to continue at Boston College after her freshman year, she took a job as a receptionist for a sports publishing company. That got her some gigs writing short articles on the New York Giants football team and served as her first entrée into what was then an exclusively man's world. She learned fast just how exclusive it was when the old boys network of sports writers shut her out of the press box at the stadium. She persisted and at least managed to get access to a separate box from the men. Dawn stood up for what she wanted and did so while battling her own issues of low self-esteem and an inner voice that constantly told her, "You're never going to make it."

In her candid and unsparing autobiography, *They Can Kill You, But They Can't Eat You*, Dawn lays out what she learned in plain-spoken prose: "This is the story of a woman who climbed the male ladder of success. A woman who learned that you cannot expect anyone to rescue or take care of you."

When a friend told her about a job opening at *Penthouse*, a British girlie magazine launching in the US market, she interviewed and was hired to write sexy and sexist advertising. She was too embarrassed to tell her parents she had landed a job with *Penthouse,* so she told them she worked for the French women's magazine *Mademoiselle.*

While critics condemned *Penthouse* as a misogynistic exploiter of women, much like its slightly more classy competitor *Playboy*, the *Penthouse* workplace, ironically, promoted women far better than most other businesses at the time. Dawn got promoted too and was soon tapped to head up the mail order merchandising department. That new assignment had her scouring sex stores in the US and Europe for sexy products that *Penthouse* could promote. One of her best sellers was a knitted "Banana Warmer" that came with a tagline she had created: "For the man who has everything and nowhere to put it." All sizes were marked "extra large." Dawn loved her job, and it introduced her to a wider circle of up-and-comers in the city.

As the head of merchandising, Dawn was to receive a "net of the profits" for the products sold in addition to a modest salary. The products she picked sold extremely well—so well that she asked *Penthouse* publisher Bob Guccione for a raise. He referred her to the accounting department, which, after a review, said that she owed *them* money—$225,000. Accounting claimed the expenses related to buying, promoting, and selling the sex toys far exceeded the revenue she brought in. The accounting trick taught her an early lesson that her mother had warned her about—never agree to a net profits deal because accountants can make them vanish. Only take a percentage of the gross revenue.

Frustrated, she quit and started a mail-order business with her first husband to sell amaryllis plants that resembled penises. Her tagline: "Grow Your Own Penis. All it takes is $6.98 and a lot of love." She bought the plants for 30 cents, sold lots, and netted a healthy profit margin that she could keep. Soon, she was making over $100,000 a year, a considerable income in the early 1970s.

By the time the business had run its course and after fighting lawsuits from Guccione over copyright issues for other products, a friend called Dawn from Los Angeles. He was a junior production manager at Paramount Pictures and asked if she might want to work for them merchandising products tied to movies. While intrigued, Dawn pointed out her rather narrow field of merchandising experience. The friend assured her, "You know, if you can merchandise the smut at Penthouse, then you can merchandise the movie business." She flew out to L.A. and was hired. One of her first big accomplishments was getting dozens of companies to pay royalties to sell toys and logos linked to the movie *Star Trek: The Motion Picture*. Notably, she convinced Coca-Cola and McDonalds to pay Paramount to use Star Trek Klingons to drink Coke and eat burgers.

Dawn's success led to a big promotion as Vice President of Production at Paramount. Before signing on, she reminded her boss, Michael Eisner, that she knew nothing about making movies, but he assured her, "Neither does anyone else." She learned fast and produced a string of hits and rose to become President of Production before the cutthroat ways of Hollywood caught up and pushed her to the side. As one door closed, another opened. Columbia Pictures was looking for a new president. She interviewed and landed the job. But Columbia was struggling, and before Dawn was able to produce more hits, Sony took over and made it clear she had to leave.

Once again, one door closed, another opened, and Dawn moved to Disney as a contractor but with far less status and power than she had at Paramount or Columbia. At least she was in her element and had the trust and confidence of those at the top. Disney badly needed a hit but couldn't afford any big-budget productions. The studio also had a reputation for being stingy, paying the least of any major studio to make movies. One day, Dawn came across the *Blue Maaga* script sandwiched in with scores of others.

Dawn had watched on TV when the Jamaican bobsled team raced and crashed at the 1988 Winter Olympics. She knew about the heartfelt, quixotic Jamaican effort to make it as bobsledders. As someone who came from a lower middle-class family and defied the odds to become the president of Columbia Pictures, she connected with the story of striving to make it big even when everyone is saying you can't do it.

More importantly, Dawn saw the potential for a movie drama about Jamaicans in the violent shanty towns of Jamaica going all-out to become Olympic bobsledders. But she felt the script by Lynn Siefert didn't quite click and handed it to writers Tommy Swerdlow and Michael Goldberg to be reworked. The new writers gave it a comedy angle that Dawn and other studio executives saw as more sellable. The name was changed from the cryptic *Blue Maaga* to a more lighthearted and relatable *Cool Runnings*, a phrase that Jamaicans use when wishing someone "safe journey" or "all the best."

CHAPTER 29

MAKING THE MOVIE

The new version of the script started with a Jamaican sprint contender for the Olympics being tripped along with two other runners while competing in the team selection trials. Frustrated at being disqualified and seeing his Olympic dream shattered, he finds out about an attempt 20 years earlier to recruit his father, who was also a sprinter, to form a bobsled team. He decides to revive the idea with his other disqualified buddies and recruits a push-cart champion to join them. By chance, they learn that an Olympic bobsled coach, who had been booted out of the federation because of cheating, lives in Kingston. Together, they approach and persuade the reluctant, alcoholic coach to create a bobsled team. Despite facing numerous comical obstacles, they somehow make it to the Olympics in Calgary and even contend for a possible medal before crashing. Despite the crash and disqualification, they become champions of the heart as the underdogs who gave it their all.

Dawn approached several top movie directors, who all turned down the chance to make *Cool Runnings*, either because they decided to take on other movie projects with more promise or because Disney couldn't pay enough. Disney had budgeted only $15 million to make *Cool Runnings*, low-end by Hollywood standards. Finally, Dawn showed the script to Jon Turteltaub, a budding director still in his twenties and just a few years out of film school. He saw potential in the script and signed on.

To prep herself for producing the movie, Dawn met with Tal, Chris, and Devon in Calgary to talk about their experience and get a better feel for their amazing foray into the sport of bobsledding. They found Dawn to be highly energetic and engaging. Her breakfast with Tal and Chris stretched three hours into lunch as she took copious notes. At the end, she said, "I loved you guys from the moment I saw you in Calgary {during the 1988 Games}. You're all fantastic, and I'm going to make you big stars!"

Dawn attempted to sign big-name Hollywood stars to play the Jamaican bobsledders. She approached Denzel Washington, Eddie Murphy, Wesley Snipes, Marlon Wayne, Cuba Gooding Jr., Jeffrey Wright, and Eric Lasade. All declined. One star actor who didn't turn down the chance to play the disgraced coach, Irv Blitzer, was John Candy. He read the script and knew right away that it would be a hit. Candy was not Disney's first choice for the Blitzer role. Kurt Russell was, but Candy persisted in getting the nod and sweetened the deal by taking a pay cut from his usual fee.

Dawn and Turteltaub still had to find the other lead actors to play the Jamaican bobsledders and went to open auditions. Four actors made the final cut, three of them Americans with varying Jamaican heritage and one Trinidadian. Dawn tapped Leon Robinson to play Derice Bannock, the cool, confident, and good-looking team captain. He had already had some success in supporting roles in major films. Doug E. Doug got the part of Sanka Coffee who said the most memorable line in the movie: "Feel the rhythm! Feel the rhyme! Get on up, it's bobsled time!" Malik Yoba was chosen to play the part of Yul Brenner, the tough guy on the team. At the audition, Yoba belted out a line from a song he had written the previous day: "Folks saying oh, they can't believe Jamaica, we have a bobsled team." Impressed, Disney hired him on the spot.

Rawle Lewis from Trinidad, the only non-American, had very little acting experience before landing the role of the shy Junior Bevil. Initially, Disney had hired him to read the script with the actors auditioning for the parts and specifically told him he would not be considered for a part. Casting directors also asked him to coach the three selected actors to speak with Jamaican accents, even after he told them he was from Trinidad.

Apparently, just being black with some kind of Caribbean accent was good enough. After three weeks, casting directors let him audition, and Dawn gave him the part.

Filming commenced in 1992 in Jamaica and Calgary. During the rehearsals, the bobsled actors all spoke their lines with raw Jamaican accents that frustrated Disney boss Jeffrey Katzenberg. He feared the "authenticity" would not be understandable to the American audience and told Turteltaub to have actors tone down the accent. The Disney executive wanted them to speak more like Sebastian the Crab's easy-to-understand West Indian accent in *The Little Mermaid*. Rather than use some directorial reason for the actors to change their accent, Turteltaub quietly pulled the actors aside and said, "I'm going to get fired if you don't sound like Sebastian." The actors got the playful hint and laughed out loud, no doubt relishing the irony of them having to develop Jamaican accents that proved to be too good. By softening their accents, they mollified Katzenberg and likely saved Turteltaub's job.

The chemistry clicked between all the actors and the director. In particular, everyone loved working with a big-name star like Candy. They found him not only wonderfully funny but exceptionally generous with his time on and off the set. Once, when the director called for a shot to be retaken at the top of the Olympic bobsled track in Calgary, John Candy was not around and could not be reached. It turned out Candy had taken time during the break to visit a children's hospital in Calgary and talk to some of the terminally ill kids.

Actors without any reputation almost never have any say over the script, but this time they did. When a scene called for the four bobsled actors to build a snowman and put a joint in its mouth, they balked. They wanted no part in reinforcing a negative stereotype of Jamaicans as druggies. The scene was quashed.

When interviewed after the movie was made, Turteltaub put it this way: "[The film's legacy is] the notion that not only can David beat Goliath, but he can have a great time doing it. And that your sense of humor and your ability to laugh is a weapon that you have that not enough people use. For us, the movie was about dignity. And with all of its silliness, dignity is at the heart of every scene of that movie."

Robinson also had a positive perspective on the movie, stating the following in an interview: "Everyone can relate to a fish-out-of-water story. Everyone can imagine what it's like to be the only one of your kind some place. That is something that universally everyone identifies with. Then it's also the message about pride, pride in your country and who you are, and about working hard to achieve the things you want."

CHAPTER 30

REACTIONS

Cool Runnings *cast a massive shadow over my life. There's a very uncomfortable position of actually being alive to watch your legacy unfold. Most people die before their legacy is revealed, but I've had to live it.*

—Tal Stokes

Disney released *Cool Runnings* on October 1, 1993, and it became an instant worldwide hit, grossing $154 million. Dawn came through for Disney, which put her back on top of her game. The film took on a number of different comical names in other countries. In Italy, the movie was called *Quattro Sottozero* ("Four Below Zero"). In France, they called it *The Rasta Rocket,* and in Norway, *Kalde Rumper* ("Cold Butts").

Most people in Jamaica liked the movie and its uplifting message, even if a little hokey. Jamaicans, of course, knew it was not a true representation of what actually happened, as they had followed the plight of their bobsledders quite closely once they reached the Olympics. People outside Jamaica didn't have the same reference point, however, and many took the movie to be a largely true story.

The highly fictionalized film didn't upset the real bobsledders either, with the exception of Tal. He watched one of the premieres in Kingston and walked out upset. For him, the movie made the sledders out to be silly and superficial, the very image he and the others had struggled so hard against. At the same time, the movie bolstered his motivation to master the sport on a world-class level. If nothing else, Tal wanted to distinguish himself from what he perceived to be the farcical portrayal of serious athletes.

Chris had a different take. After watching *Cool Runnings* with his friends back in Moscow, Idaho, he became excited and also motivated. Indeed, the movie resolved uncertainties he had wrestled with about whether to commit to a career in education administration or continue bobsledding. The film answered his dilemma. At the same time, Chris noted that friends and colleagues began treating him differently, showing him a degree of deference that made him uncomfortable. They all made him realize that he was now part of something special.

In *Cool Runnings and Beyond*, Chris wrote, "Over the years, I have heard a sentiment expressed by some that the movie sought to make fun of us. I disagree entirely. In fact, I am certain that the movie was done with the object of building us up, not breaking us down, and of acknowledging the humor in the story, without going to the ridiculous . . . While the movie was not an exact history, it certainly captured the spirit of Jamaican Bobsleigh."

Altering truth and shaping perceptions to make a story more compelling is, of course, the currency of Hollywood. Writers, producers, and directors are all under pressure to visually tell a relatable story on the screen that brings in paying audiences and generates cash for the studio and investors. That reality was reflected in *Cool Runnings*. A few of the differences between Hollywood's version of events and what actually happened are worth noting:

The movie tried to link pushcart racing in Jamaica with bobsled driving, but the two have nothing in common. Pushcart racing skill was never a factor in the selection of bobsled athletes.

The crash in the four-man sled was caused by speed and driver inexperience, not mechanical failure.

In the movie, the coach was made out to be a disgraced drunk, but there was no such person associated with the team.

The bar scene where the East German bobsledder tells the Jamaicans to go back to their "tourist island" never happened. In fact, the East Germans, along with other international bobsledders, welcomed the Jamaican entry, even if they questioned their readiness. But good stories need a bad guy antagonist, and East Germany, a country that no longer existed when the movie was made, served that purpose.

Ironically, the movie that got the story of the Jamaican bobsledders so wrong turned out to be a fund-raising bonus for the real Jamaican bobsledders, as it kept their profile high. Indeed, the fanciful journey of the real 1988 Jamaican bobsledders, combined with the fictional movie, sharply elevated global interest in Olympic bobsledding. Until the Jamaican bobsled team, followed by *Cool Runnings*, bobsledding had been a fringe sport in the Winter Games. Distressingly, for all the international popularity generated for the sport, as well as the profits made by the movie, the Jamaican bobsledders received very little and nothing close to what they deserved.

The Disney contract negotiated by George was to pay him, his wife, Will, and five members of the team a total of $225,000 for the rights to make the movie. Thirty-five thousand dollars was to be paid at the signing, with the balance forthcoming once filming began. While welcome, the money, once divided up, came nowhere near covering the costs of even going to the Olympics. As is the case with most Olympic athletes, the Jamaicans fell into considerable debt after Calgary that took years to clear.

The contract also had a clause to pay 1.5% of the "profits" made by the movie to the group. But, as Dawn had learned the hard way while selling sex products for *Penthouse* Magazine, net profits have a way of vanishing when accountants add up expenses. George, Will, and all the Jamaican bobsledders fell into that trap and never received any percentage, even though *Cool Runnings* made an enormous amount of money and cost relatively little to film. The bitterness of being ripped off hit hard and would linger for decades.

Meanwhile, movie audiences filled theaters and cheered the lovable characters who held their heads (and sled) high after crashing. Outside the public eye, real Jamaican bobsledders quietly prepared to beat the best.

PART FIVE

ALL DOWNHILL

CHAPTER 31

SLIDING TO LILLEHAMMER OLYMPICS '94

Norway won the bid to host the 1994 Winter Olympics, which would take place in the small town of Lillehammer, 84 miles (134 km) north of Oslo. The IOC vote in 1987 to stagger the Summer and Winter Olympics so they would take place two years apart instead of the same year was a welcome decision for the Jamaicans. But the opportunity to take part in a third Olympics sooner also compressed the time to prepare to just two years.

The FIBT implemented even stricter qualifying criteria for the '94 Olympics. In order to make the Olympic roster, a national team had to enter five sanctioned races on three different tracks over a two-year period. The intent of the regulation was to reduce the number of unprepared teams showing up to compete by requiring more race experience. The FIBT called it the "5-3-2 Rule," which was also informally known as the "Jamaican Rule" due to the prominence of the 1988 crash. It did not matter that the Jamaicans had improved substantially or that many other teams entered the competition with far less capability. The Jamaicans shrugged off the label even though it kept alive the notion that they shouldn't be in the bobsled game.

After one disastrous and one substandard Olympics, it would have been easy for Tal and his teammates to walk away from bobsledding, knowing they tried hard and had given their best. But Tal, more stubborn than the others, was not about to bow out—even with the short readiness window for the next Winter Olympics, the more demanding qualifying rules, and the perennial struggle for funding. Tal brushed off the momentary misgivings he had shared with Chris about black people not being able to be bobsledders. He reached deep into the reservoir of confidence built since childhood—the spunk and mettle that always kept him focused on the task at hand until mastered. Still, the practicalities of pulling off another Jamaican Olympic bobsled pursuit loomed even larger and raised more doubts about becoming competitive.

Tal had seen up close how the best-funded European bobsledders could afford the fastest sleds and the biggest support staff that consistently brought them medals. The glaring gulf between the wealth-driven teams in Europe and the cash-poor teams like Jamaica reinforced a daunting, immutable fact: No matter how hard the Jamaicans aspired to be the Cinderella team, the David vs. Goliath, the underdogs who compensated for their shortage of talent with an abundance of grit—cold cash made the difference between those who stood on the podium and who sat in the stands. Tal made the call to press on anyhow.

In 1992, Leo took over the reins from Will as president of the Jamaican Bobsleigh Federation. His military logistics background, MBA, and natural organizational skills made him a perfect choice. Leo had also been Deputy *Chef de Mission* in Albertville and followed the trajectory of Jamaican bobsledding since 1988. He grasped the challenges they faced from the moment he stepped into the job. Notably, he too understood that Jamaica's superb athletes were not enough to make them a real bobsled nation, and he committed to setting up the best administration they could afford. It would also take a big burden off Tal, who had handled most of the logistics, and let him focus more on driving the sled.

Leo was also passionate about branding Team Jamaica by capitalizing on the publicity from the movie that had decidedly boosted the ongoing worldwide fascination with the bobsledders from Jamaica. Instead of just asking for money from sponsors, he worked out a marketing plan to "sell" the brand as a business tool to improve corporate sales. Leo also expanded the media interviews with the bobsledders to keep the story fresh and their faces out there. Recognizing Tal's hard-to-hide disinterest in the public image side, Leo sat down and coached him. He even drew up a list of the frequent "dumb" questions the TV talking heads would ask and provided Tal with a straightforward, short answer to each one.

When the Tourist Board sent Tal to New York City to appear on one of the morning TV shows, he was shown to a dressing room that would powder him up for the cameras. By chance, he was put in the same dressing room as former President Richard Nixon, who was getting ready for his own TV appearance. On seeing Tal enter, President Nixon stood up, extended his hand, and formally introduced himself, saying, "Hello, I'm former President Richard Nixon," as if he might not be recognizable. A rather surprised Tal shook hands and introduced himself as the captain of the Jamaican bobsled team. Nixon said that he had heard about the team and wished Tal well before leaving.

When Coach Pete's contract ended after the Games in Albertville, the Jamaicans were once again on their own. But they were also four years savvier and knew what to do. And they had Sepp to keep them on track and coax his coaching friends to give out pointers during training. Still, the Jamaicans needed to bring in more talent and find a full-time coach if they were ever going to reach a higher level.

Always a dependable and solid bobsled supporter, Col. Barnes reached out to the JDF to find and encourage the best athletes to show up for the fall 1992 tryouts. Of the soldiers dispatched, Pvt. Winston Watt clearly excelled. He was the JDF shot put champion, as well as an outstanding soccer player and phenomenal sprinter who could bench press 400 lbs.

Alcan, the bauxite company and a 1992 team sponsor, also submitted a top candidate for consideration, Wayne Thomas. Wayne easily won the sprint events at the trials and matched Winston's bench press with a 700 lb squat, proving that he too had the right stuff to be an exceptional pusher/brakeman.

Pvt. Jerome Lewis also tried out and made the cut. Jerome drove big trucks for the JDF, a skill that would come in handy when the team transported their sleds around Europe while competing in qualifying events.

Tal, Chris, Ricky, Winston, Wayne, and Jerome went straight into training for Lillehammer. Devon and Michael opted out of the Olympics this time. The three experienced bobsledders from 1988 and 1992 helped guide the three newcomers through workouts and drills, first in Jamaica and then on tracks in Europe and North America. Tal and Chris focused on training and racing, while Leo oversaw the management of logistics and scheduling.

In late 1992, Chris's good friend from Norway and fellow student-athlete at the University of Idaho, Trond Knaplund, called. He told him the Lillehammer Olympic Organizing Committee (LOOC) had put him in charge of managing the newly built bobsled course. In that capacity, he invited the Jamaicans to come try it out in January 1993. Unfortunately, the Jamaica Bobsleigh Federation had run out of money. But Tal was intent on taking Trond up on the offer and borrowed $5000 in cash from a personal friend in Jamaica to travel to Norway. Trond kindly let him stay in his house in Lillehammer to keep expenses down.

FIBT rules technically restricted the foreign teams of sliders to one International Training Week prior to the Olympics. The intent was to preclude foreign bobsled teams from having an unfair advantage by becoming too familiar with the track. The Norwegians, however, would not be entering a bobsled team in the '94 Olympics and, thus, would have no "home team." Several Norwegian bobsled clubs trained on the track nonetheless, and Trond arranged for Tal to train as part of a club while relishing the winter wonderland of Lillehammer.

Before building the track located in the village of Hundefossen, nine miles (15 km) from Lillehammer, the Norwegians carefully considered the environmental impact of a bobsled course in multiple locations. Rather than constructing a raised track, like most other modern courses, they designed one that followed the natural contours of the mountain slope. The Norwegians also shaped the curves and built the roof over part of the track from the trees they had cut down, thus incorporating the same wood back into the mountainside.

After nearly a month of good training runs in Lillehammer, Tal and the team still faced the challenge of meeting the FIBT's new 5-3-2 competition criteria and earning points to qualify for the '94 Olympics. In the fall of 1993, the Jamaican Tourist Board came through with another sponsorship grant, as did Red Stripe with $75,000 in sponsorship money. The good news essentially relieved them of the immediate financial hardship that had stalked them since the beginning and allowed them to enter qualifying races. However, they would soon face a new stress in their pursuit of securing an Olympic spot at Lillehammer '94.

CHAPTER 32

OFF-BEAT COACH
TAKES CHARGE

During one of the last qualifying events in Calgary in early December 1993, the Jamaican team gathered for dinner at a McDonald's restaurant. Halfway through the meal, an excited man, filled with nervous energy and looking to be in his mid-thirties, approached the table. Wearing sweatpants and a sweatshirt, he introduced himself as Sam Bock from Montreal and launched into a monologue detailing his background as a personal coach to one of the top Canadian bobsled teams. He rambled on about the athletes he had trained that had set push-start records, how he built the fastest two-man sled ever to race on the Calgary track, and the benefits of his unique nutrition program that were better than taking steroids. He even gave the Jamaicans a quick tutorial on optimizing the push by demonstrating slight changes to the body position. After talking non-stop for 15 minutes, standing the whole time, he ended by saying the Jamaican team had impressed him with their excellent start times at the 1988 Calgary Olympics and offered to be their coach.

Nobody was quite sure what to make of this guy who appeared from nowhere, but it was clear he knew what he was talking about. Back in Jamaica, Tal and Chris told Leo about Sam's out-of-the-blue pitch to be coach and asked if he should be considered. Leo said he had heard about Sam and confirmed that his credentials checked out. Sam did indeed have a reputation in Canada as a top coach. He had also studied to become a nuclear engineer and displayed exceptional technical brilliance in every project he took on. However, Leo had also heard that he came with "baggage." No one knew what that meant. But since all the other top coaches had declined offers to coach, the Jamaicans decided to take a chance on retaining Sam. They had six weeks to go before the Norwegian Crown Prince would light the Lillehammer '94 Olympic flame.

Coach Sam didn't waste any time taking over the team and laid out an intense training schedule. He immediately moved the team to a special push-training facility in the former East German town of Oberhof, where they trained eight hours a day in isolation. The Jamaicans were actually the first non-East German team to use the advanced facility. Coach Sam, who would be tagged with the nickname "Sambo," called all the shots and brooked no dissent or questioning of his methodology. He knew what needed to be done. Still, Coach Sam's demanding and, at times, seemingly disrespectful manner grated deeply, as it ran counter to the cultural sensibilities of Jamaican masculinity. From the start, Sam's perceived lack of "respect," however unintentional in his mind, lit a slow fuse of resentment.

No deviation from the agenda was too trivial to set Coach Sam on a tear. Once, he saw Chris about to eat a hamburger at the train station and ripped the white bread buns out of Chris's hands. After throwing the buns on the track, Coach Sam launched into a tirade to a bewildered Chris about the evils of white bread and the negative effects on the body.

Indeed, Coach Sam insisted the team follow a special diet that was heavy on healthy fats, such as omega-3 oils. By applying a strict "good" fat diet, Coach Sam sought to speed up recovery from injuries, supplemented with physical therapy. Notably, Coach Sam reinforced his belief that proper diet and vitamins, rigorously enforced, obviated the need for performance-enhancing drugs that some top athletes, including bobsledders, used to gain a critical edge. Coach Sam based much of his approach on books by Udo Rasmussen and Nobel Prize Laureate Linus Pauling, which appealed to Tal's intellectual sense of fitness and recovery through food. Other members of the team, however, had a more skeptical view of what they saw as Coach Sam's nutrition fanaticism.

Coach Sam also put the Jamaicans on a tough training regimen that began at 8:00 a.m. sharp with two hours of running sprints on the track. After a one-hour rest, they would practice pushing sleds on the push-track for an hour and a half. The team would get an hour and a half break before proceeding to the gym for another hour and a half of weight lifting. The intensity would be altered between one hard day and one easy day. Tal saw his times in the 30-meter sprints go down from 4.11 seconds to 3.89 seconds.

Coach Sam also tinkered with the two DDG sleds that Tal had acquired. But this time, there were no freebie sleds in exchange for publicity. Karola Bräer charged the Jamaicans cash to rent them. Notably, Sam raised the push handles a few inches to match the height of the pushers and thereby enhance their effectiveness. The adjustment also meant that the push bars did not come all the way down into the slots after loading. At the time, this was legal. But that wouldn't stop other bobsledders later on from complaining that the adjusted push bars gave the sled a slight aerodynamic advantage. FIBT allowed the Jamaicans to compete. The following year, however, the FIBT would ban adjusting the push bar heights.

The last week of training at Oberhoff focused on selecting who would be the pusher/brakeman for the two-man sled and pushers/brakeman for the four-man sled. Tal expected Chris to once again be his pusher/brakeman for the two-man, but Wayne proved to be the better athlete for the position by winning most of the push-offs. However, Wayne had also pulled a hamstring in the course of the hard training. Rather than have Wayne take time to recover, Coach Sam asked Wayne to work through the injury. Coach Sam's unconventional philosophy held that an athlete could channel the pain of the injury into greater focus on performance. Tal, as the captain and pilot, could have chosen Chris anyhow, but Chris stepped in and told Tal, "Wayne is your man," despite the injury. Selection for who would push for the four-man sled with Tal would come later.

In January 1994, the Jamaicans raced in the World Cup in La Plagne for the final qualification points and easily made the cut for the Olympics. While competing at La Plagne, the team had Red Stripe logos painted on the top and sides of the four-man sled as part of the sponsorship deal. They then shipped the sled to Lillehammer. The team felt stronger and more confident, due in large part to Sam's relentless and often ruthless approach to workouts and what the body consumed. Notably, the new pushers, Wayne and Winston, readily took to bobsledding and kept getting better—athletically, technically, and logistically. Tal could entrust them with properly prepping the sled before a start, which relieved him of most of that crucial task. The confidence was so high that Tal and Chris believed that, for the first time, they had a real bobsled team.

CHAPTER 33

A COSTLY MISTAKE

The Lillehammer Winter Games opened on February 12, 1994, at the Lysgårdsbakken ski jump arena on a bitterly cold night. Chris carried the Jamaican flag to the lively cheers of the spectators as the team joined the other Olympians in the stands at the base of the slope. Tal chose not to participate in the opening ceremonies to avoid the fatigue of marching and standing for hours. He, like some of the other athletes, skipped the pageantry of the Games to focus, even if his two-man race would not begin for another week on February 19 and 20. He really didn't care much for the circus-like spectacle anyhow.

After all the nations had assembled and officials gave speeches, the lights dimmed. A Norwegian ethnic Sámi welcomed the visitors with a solo of a traditional *joik*, or a "story chant," handed down through centuries. The Sámi are an indigenous, nomadic people with Asiatic roots who roamed the far north, known sometimes as Lapland, for thousands of years as reindeer herders. Following the mesmerizing *joik* of these ancient people, dozens of fiddlers on skis crawled out from under the snow of the slope and skied down together, "Telemark" style, while playing a traditional Norwegian folk tune.

The most epic Olympic torch-lighting ceremony in any Winter Games came when ski jumper Stein Gruben was handed the torch at the top of the ski jump. As a light snow fell, Gruben lifted himself slowly off the start bar, Norwegian ice water running through his veins, and skied down the ramp. He hit the jump perfectly and lifted the flaming torch high while soaring through the air to the roars of the crowd. After landing perfectly, he handed off the torch to ignite the nearby cauldron. Gruben wasn't supposed to do the torch jump. Two days before the opening ceremonies, the first designated torch jumper had injured himself during practice. So it fell to Gruben, who had not even been selected for the Norwegian Olympic ski-jumping team, to get it right in 48 hours for the cameras and a billion people watching.

Among those watching the opening ceremony was First Lady Hillary Clinton, who headed the American Presidential Delegation. In the course of traveling from Oslo to Lillehammer, her security detail included Norwegian policemen. Impressed by their professionalism, courtesy, and especially good looks, Mrs. Clinton supposedly remarked, "If you get stopped by a Norwegian policeman, be thankful."

The small town of Lillehammer, with a population of just under 24,000 and not even a proper resort town, built a single Olympic Village for nearly all 1,738 athletes, as well as provided lodging for thousands of media representatives and visitors. The locus of activity in one town allowed for much more face-to-face exchange between athletes and visitors, which had been missing during the Albertville Olympics. The Jamaicans settled comfortably into the town, particularly Tal, who had spent time sliding down the track a year before. Still on a high since the final qualifying race in La Plagne, they had a newfound confidence that dared them to believe they could finish in the top tier, if not the podium itself.

Two other athletes also settled into Lillehammer: America's leading figure skaters, Nancy Kerrigan and Tonya Harding. One month earlier, just before the United States Figure Skating Championships, Kerrigan was attacked and struck with a baton across her lower right thigh. The attack and injury sustained by a then unknown assailant forced her to withdraw from the championships, which Harding then easily won. Kerrigan recovered in time to participate in the Lillehammer Olympics, but suspicions mounted that Harding may have played a role in the attack and cast a dark shadow over the Olympic figure skating event. Kerrigan would win silver, while Harding came in 8th. Later, Harding's ex-husband and three others were convicted of attacking or conspiring to attack Kerrigan and were given prison sentences. Harding only admitted to knowledge of the attack after it took place and pled guilty to conspiring to hinder prosecution, for which she was given probation and a stiff fine. She was also banned for life from the United States Figure Skating Association.

The American bobsled team, meanwhile, was intent as ever on ending its ever-lengthening Olympic medal drought, now extending to 38 years. This time, they brought their own brand-new American Bo-Dyn sleds. Motivated by the disappointing results of the American team in 1992, NASCAR legend Geoff Bodine teamed up with engineers from Chassis Dynamics, a top US race car builder, to develop "Bo-Dyn" (combining Bodine and Chassis Dynamics) sleds specifically for American bobsledders. Bo-Dyn stripped down the sleds and assessed how each component could be adjusted or changed out quickly to suit changing conditions or driver preferences. Most importantly, the Bo-Dyn project involved actual bobsledders giving feedback. Bodine invested his savings, while the builders went without pay for months, to develop a top-notch bobsled.

Initially, the Bo-Dyn team received a cool reception from much of the skeptical and notoriously tight circle of Lake Placid bobsledders. They had seen their share of American bobsled-building dreamers come and go. One of the early believers who bucked the doubters and helped move the project forward was TV commentator John Morgan. With the Bo-Dyn sleds, the Americans might have a chance to break the domination of German and Swiss teams that had sucked up almost all the Olympic medals for nearly 40 years. Bo-Dyn's day would come but not in Lillehammer.

As the Jamaicans prepped their DDG sleds for training runs before the two-man race, other bobsledders had become noticeably less friendly with them. The previous encouragement by fellow competitors was replaced with a hint of tension reserved for serious challengers, which the Jamaicans took as a subtle compliment. Most of the experienced teams had observed the improvement of the Jamaican team over the past year at World Cup qualifying events. The pushers clocked quicker starts, Tal steered better lines down the track, and the sleds reached the bottom faster. Leading up to the Games, Tal had begun holding the steering rope D-rings with just two bare fingers to improve sensitivity and let the runners "talk" to him.

But anything that could go wrong for the Jamaican two-man would go wrong.

*   *   *

The day before the first two heats of the two-man race, Wayne continued to complain about a painful hamstring injury that might affect his pushing power. Tal discussed with Coach Sam whether Chris should come back and replace Wayne as pusher. Tal leaned towards Chris but wanted to sleep on it before making the call. That night, Tal agonized over what to do. The next morning, Tal decided to stick with Wayne, as he was still a formidable athlete even with an injury.

On the first run of the two-man, the team placed 25th out of 43 teams. On the second run, Tal and Wayne moved up a notch to 24th place, even with a slightly slower time. It wasn't a sterling performance, but not bad for the first day, and better than Albertville or Calgary.

After moving the sled off the track, an FIBT official tapped Tal on the shoulder and said the Jamaican sled had been selected for weighing. These weighings are random, and all sledders and technical teams prepare for that possibility by ensuring the combined weight of their two-man sled with crew does not exceed 360 kilos. Unconcerned, Tal and Wayne moved the sled to the scale and watched, confident they would come in under the maximum. After training the previous evening, Sam had weighed the sled and noted that it was at least a kilo below the maximum limit when combined with the weight of both sledders.

To everyone's horror, the hand of the scale moved just beyond the 360 kilo mark, fluttering a bit, and then steadied to show 300 grams over the limit. Officials immediately disqualified Jamaica. Nobody understood how this could happen. Wayne, who sometimes did put on weight from one day to the next, thought he might be the culprit. But he weighed the same as the day before, as did Tal.

Very quickly, the Jamaicans were back in the news for another befuddlement. Even Jamaica's main newspaper, now called *The Gleaner*, would print a caricature of Wayne with a large potbelly from drinking too much Red Stripe. Leo ended up taking the brunt of the criticism for the national embarrassment. He tried to minimize the incident by explaining that they were really there for the four-man event. The skeptics, of course, now had one more confirmation of Jamaican unsuitability for bobsledding. And once more, they would be called a collection of perennial wannabes who couldn't even keep the sled and team within FIBT weight limits. The naysayers even hinted that Jamaica's improving performance was due to the slight extra weight, not because of any talent.

It turned out that the night before the race, Tal had made a decision to change the sled runners to ones that would perform better in the colder temperatures. The move made sense, but the new runners weighed slightly more than the original ones, which accounted for the weight difference. While Tal blamed himself and took responsibility, everyone should have paid more attention. A mix-up of a seemingly innocuous but critical detail led to a calamitous mistake that knocked out Team Jamaica with a stinging DQ next to the name. The maddening humiliation also underscored the overriding importance of race management in bobsledding. Jamaica would not be the only team to make a monumental disqualifying error due to equipment in Lillehammer.

The two Swiss teams, driven by Gustav Weder and Reto Götchi, won the gold and silver after battling it out with the Italian team that came in third. The Swiss victory was bittersweet, however, as the pushers for each team, Donat and Guido Acklin, were brothers. Germany came in fourth, marking the first time in 30 years a German team had been denied a medal in the two-man event. The Americans, too, failed to meet expectations with disappointing 13th and 14th place finishes.

Tal wasted no time agonizing over the embarrassing and painful two-man sled mishap. All eyes turned to the four-man race set for the following weekend of February 26 and 27. The Jamaicans had to do well, not just finish. And they would be going up against the strongest field of medal contenders ever from powerhouse Europe as well as the US and Canada.

CHAPTER 34

ONE MINUTE
FROM REDEMPTION

Bobsleigh is the kind of sport that most parallels life.
At its core, it is you against the track. Just as in life, it is you against
the world. If you are looking for competitive inspiration from others,
then you are limited to what they are.

—Tal Stokes

The Jamaicans opened the crate containing their four-man sled that had been shipped from La Plagne and moved it to the loading dock to make some technical adjustments. TV news crews milled about filming them, but nobody asked questions. An FIBT official happened to pass by and noticed the Red Stripe logos on the hull. He told them the logos had to be removed, citing the IOC prohibition against advertisements on sleds (though allowed in World Cup competitions). In fact, the Jamaicans fully understood the requirement and were about to remove the signage to comply, as other bobsledders had already done to their sleds.

That should have been the end of it. While watching TV that night, however, the Jamaicans were shocked to see a story about the IOC "warning" them about removing branding images from their sleds, along with footage from the morning showing the Red Stripe logos. Clearly, the Jamaicans had been singled out for negative coverage. Mike Fennel saw the TV report and immediately called Leo to pointedly tell him that the Jamaica Olympic Association could easily be sanctioned for the infraction. Coming off the two-man sled disqualification, they did not need yet another piece of negative publicity that suggested they were somehow trying to skirt the rules.

The cloud passed, and the Jamaicans could refocus on the competition. They still had a good feeling about their chances in Lillehammer, especially after coming in 6th place twice during training runs. Though the training runs were not all-out races, the informal times nonetheless served as an indicator of readiness. Sam was particularly excited and worked non-stop to make sure every technical piece was in order. Wayne, by then, had overcome most of his hamstring injury thanks to team doctor Dr. John Sandell, a chiropractor and acupuncturist Chris knew well from his days at the University of Idaho. The hamstring injury, which should have taken two weeks to heal, healed in just a few days.

On the morning of race day, Tal went to the top of the course, walked down the track, and mentally rehearsed sliding through every curve and straightaway. He took out a stopwatch and timed his imaginary run, clocking himself at 52.51 seconds. As a final preparation, he walked into the nearby Norwegian woods to be alone and meditate.

The team took the sled on a truck to the top of the track and placed it along the *fermé* (closed zone) outside the start house in the position they would race. FIBT inspectors took the runner temperatures and looked over the sled for infractions as everyone held their breath. They passed.

As each team ahead raced down the track, the Jamaicans moved their sled closer to the start area until they got the signal to slide it into place against the start blocks. Tal, Chris, Wayne, and Winston jumped up and down, hollering yelps and slapping each other until the 60-second buzzer sounded. Tal switched back into his meditative state and imagined the movements he would feel speeding down the chute. This time, he kept the demons at bay. He had no sickness or injury to worry about, no concerns about the coach, and no doubts about his ability.

Each man stood behind his push bar, fully engaged. Tal brought down his goggles and slapped his head, calling out, "One, two, three." Employing Coach Sam's push technique with hips forward, the team pushed with more power than ever, clocking 5.02 seconds over the 50-meter start zone, one of the fastest times in the Olympic competition. After everyone hopped in the sled and tucked in perfectly, Tal drove exactly the way he had visualized and finished in a time of 52.50 seconds. Just 1/100ths of a second off from what he had clocked earlier in his mind. That run put the Jamaicans in 18th place after the first heat. With that initial success, team confidence surged. Track manager Trond, an unabashed Jamaica bobsled fan, made regular loudspeaker announcements lauding their performance.

In the second heat, the Jamaicans got off to another superb Fly-Zone start with a time of 5.06 seconds and an almost as good finish time of 52.56 seconds, leaving them in 18th place for the first day of competition. The Germany II team, driven by Harald Czudaj, took the lead, followed by Switzerland's Gustav Weder and the Germany I team, driven by Wolfgang Hoppe. Czudaj's own demons from 1992, when his race entry was held up due to espionage accusations, had left him alone too. The new American Bo-Dyn Night Train sleds driven by Brian Shimer and Randy Will barely hung on 10th and 11th place, just under a second behind Czudaj. A medal was still within reach, though it was almost certainly not gold.

That evening, back at the Olympic Village, an enthusiastic Coach Sam called a team meeting. In the course of his pep talk, he told a story about a Canadian team pushing a car up the hill in Calgary just before the race that resulted in them clocking the best sled push time ever recorded over the start zone. Unwilling to let the success of the day speak for itself, the coach said he wanted everyone to push the van up the hill just before the race the next day to give them an even better start push time. The bizarre request, even by Coach Sam's unorthodox coaching standards, took the team by surprise. No one said anything. They just let it hang in the air until Coach Sam went off to bed. Chris spoke first, saying, "There will be no pushing of any van tomorrow."

The sun shined brightly the next morning as the 30 teams lined up their sleds in the starting order. When FIBT officials approached to measure the temperature of the runners, each team turned their sleds over. Concerned about how warm the sun's rays might be despite the cold air, the Jamaicans and several other teams took no chances and put up umbrellas to shade the runners.

When the FIBT officials came over to press their gauge against the runners of the USA Team I sled driven by Shiner, the reading showed the runners exceeded the 4°C limit, and the team was disqualified on the spot. Since the Jamaicans had a later start time and were, therefore, further down the queue of sleds, they had time to quickly check their own runners to make sure they stayed within the allowance. They could not afford a second DQ, which would effectively end Jamaican bobsledding. Luckily, the temperature for the runners met the legal standard, and they kept the umbrellas over them until the officials came by to measure. Once more, everyone held their breath, this time a little longer than the day before. They passed.

The heartbreaking DQ of the American sled not only ended Shimer's Lillehammer Olympics due to a critical technicality but also scaled back the Olympic trial for the new Bo-Dyn sleds. No other team in bobsled Olympic history had been disqualified for going over the runner temperature variance limit. Some in the American camp complained that maybe the French FIBT official took the temperature improperly or maybe even wanted to knock the Americans out, but there was no evidence to support these suspicions. It can be argued that the official should have just let the Americans put their sled back on the ice and then re-measured the temperature. It seemed plain that the Americans had not taken into account the sun affecting the runners in severely cold weather. If nothing else, the

DQ showed that things can go terribly wrong for the most highly experienced and capable sledders.

As the Jamaicans moved closer to the start, Sepp, the team's godfather, came over to brush the ice off their shoe spikes, a gesture of reassurance and to let them know he had confidence in them. Coach Sam, still beaming from the day before, asked if the team had pushed the van up the hill. The team told him they had no time that morning, but maybe next year.

Team Jamaica pushed an impressive start in the third heat and posted another brilliant time of 52.39 seconds. That put them in a stunning 10th place for the heat and 15th place overall when the times for the three heats were aggregated. Per FIBT regulations, the starting order would be reversed for the top 15, which meant the Jamaicans would go first in the fourth and final heat. They could not have wished for a better outcome because of the first sled's advantage of sliding on cleaner, faster ice. It also meant that the Jamaicans had to hustle quickly to get their sled back to the top to be ready to go.

Even in the hectic scramble, Tal took the time to find his isolated spot in the woods to meditate. As he stood in the crunchy snow among the pine trees, a calm came over him that took the pressure off. He was not alone, however. As chance would have it, gold medal favorite Weder had also wandered into the woods to be alone and collect his thoughts. They locked eyes but said nothing. In that stare, however, Weder conveyed to Tal unmistakable respect. In years to come, whenever Tal found that he was doubting himself, he would replay the intense two seconds when Weder's eyes bore into his. Unlike Tal that morning, Weder was not in a good space. After three runs, Weder was 11/100ths of a second behind his German rival, Czudaj. He had already calculated that, at that level of competition, the time would be too much to make up in the final heat starting in 10 minutes.

Back at the track, CBS Olympic commentators John Morgan and Sean McDonough sensed the moment as the Jamaicans moved their sled to the starting block and played a clip of the crash in Calgary in 1988. Sean noted, "It was six years since Dudley Stokes and the Jamaicans burst onto the scene in Calgary." Back then they were a likable sideshow. Some feared for their lives the way they were driving."

John followed with his own comment: "Yeah, he [Tal] had no clue about driving the big four-man sled, and this crash there [in Calgary] I thought ended his career."

Once more, Tal stood at the top of the track and peered down the frozen chute, glistening in the bright sun. As before, crowds cheered loudly and rang their cowbells for the four Jamaican bobsledders. Since *Cool Runnings* had been released four months earlier, people watching felt an even closer affinity to them. But this was no *Cool Runnings* team. Jamaicans were no longer the underdogs. A far more confident team readied themselves to race. Nothing was going to spoil the last run. In that moment, Norwegian ice water pumped through Jamaican veins.

At the buzzer, Tal, Chris, Wayne, and Winston pushed with keen awareness that redemption waited at the bottom in less than 60 seconds, if they could hold it together one more time. They built up speed over the first 15 meters before breaking the start timer beam and then kept accelerating across the 50-meter start zone. As they tucked into the sled one by one, the sounds of the crowd fell away. In the silence of their cocoon, save for the muffled rattling, they barreled down the track.

Present in the moment without thoughts and only vaguely aware of the shapes of each approaching curve, Tal peered ahead to where he needed to be. Feeling as much as seeing, he let the sled find the perfect lines, barely tweaking the steering ropes. When the Jamaicans crossed the finish line, John, the booming voice of Olympic bobsledding, belted out over the mic, "Dudley Stokes has finally figured out how to drive a sled!"

After the bobsled finally came to a stop in the braking area, Tal jumped out triumphantly. He finally let go of the pent-up emotions he had held inside for six years since Calgary and banged his hand on the top of the sled over and over in jubilation. This was Tal's finest run, the one he had earned through pain and struggle. The team clocked the 10th fastest time in the fourth heat as well—52.51 seconds. Their aggregate time of 3:29.96 minutes for all four heats earned them 14th place, just 1/100ths of a second ahead of the second American team, driven by Randy Will. They also beat vaunted sledders from France, Sweden, Japan, Latvia, Italy, and Russia for the biggest upset in bobsled history. FIBT officials rushed over to shake their hands and congratulate them, saying, "You are the future of bobsledding." At last, the Jamaicans scotched the persistent notion that had dogged them since 1988—that they were a joke and didn't deserve to be there.

Back home in Jamaica, most of the population watched the race on TV early in the morning and quickly grasped the significance of their accomplishment. People poured out into the streets, shouting with joy and honking their horns for hours. Their boys had defied steep odds and prevailed over some of the best teams in the world, including the Americans. *The Gleaner* ran a big front-page story lauding the team—a far different tone from the sports writer's scoffing tone in 1988, when the team was heading to Calgary. Every Jamaican felt a sense of pride.

Czudaj's Germany Team II held on to win the gold, while Weder's Switzerland Team I took silver. Weder had managed to gain on Czudaj by 6/100ths of a second when all the times were combined, but it was not enough, as he had predicted. The Germany Team I, driven by Hoppe, stood on the podium with a bronze. Upon returning home to New York, the driver of Team USA, Randy Will, had to endure painful taunts of "Hey, you got beat by the Jamaicans."

The team from Bosnia-Herzegovina finished in last place, but they certainly represented the Olympic spirit of inclusiveness. Racing two years after gaining independence following Yugoslavia's disintegration and while a brutal ethnic war still raged back home, the four-man team consisted of two Bosnian Muslims, an ethnic Croat, and an ethnic Serb. They used a sled donated by the Dutch. But it was the Jamaicans who captured the spotlight, not by crashing but by taking their place in the pantheon of bob-sledding's elite.

CHAPTER 35
ENOUGH!

The team's return trip to Jamaica was delayed by two weeks because of plane booking problems. So they stayed in the Lillehammer Olympic Village, where they often spoke with journalists who could not get enough interviews with them. But just before departure, Leo passed on a request by the Jamaica Tourist Board for the team to fly to New York to appear on the David Letterman show. The Tourist Board hadn't actually booked the team on the show but wanted the bobsledders to hang out in New York for a week or so to see if they could get slotted in. Tal turned down the request. He had only seen his family once for a brief 24 hours since being present for the birth of his daughter just before heading to the airport in early November.

Tal and the team flew home instead, where they received an enthusiastic reception by Jamaica's movers and shakers at the airport VIP lounge and then an exuberant greeting by Prime Minister Seaga at his residence. Jamaicans now saw the bobsledders as true heroes who proved what Jamaicans could do, not just guys who made a valiant effort in a foreign winter sport.

*   *   *

After surprising the world bobsled community in Lillehammer with their remarkable achievement, the team had good reason to be confident about their prospects at the upcoming 1998 Olympics in Nagano, Japan. Coach Sam could claim a big share of the credit for getting them to a new level and cracking the top 15. Perhaps his quirky and harsh methods of training combined with nutrition worked, though at a high emotional cost.

When the bobsled season resumed in late 1994, John Morgan and the Lake Placid bobsled community decided to organize an invitational two-man bobsled race for cash prizes. Only 15 top teams were invited, including Tal and Wayne, who had proven themselves to be in that league. Lake Placid's Mt. Van Hoevenberg Olympic Bobsled Run still maintained its reputation as the most dangerous track in the world, in large part because the curves were too sharp for the newer and faster sleds. It was so treacherous that the FIBT sought to close it to international competition. Nevertheless, the best bobsledders from around the world showed up for a rare opportunity to win money in their sport. At first, the Lake Placid organizers wanted to award cash only to the top three who made the podium, but Britain's best bobsledder, Mark Tout, suggested that half of the award money be split evenly among those who did not make the podium. The organizers agreed. A few years earlier, much of Mark's face had been ripped off during a crash on this track, but it didn't deter him from coming back to compete.

After a few practice runs, seven of the teams decided the track was too risky and dropped out. But Tal stayed to slide on the track that he knew well and had one of the best races of his life, even on par with Lillehammer. With the mojo still going, he and Wayne placed fourth in the group and took home a share of the prize money. More importantly, he reconfirmed Jamaica's new place among the bobsledding powers. The exhilaration would not last long.

Even before the World Cup qualifying races, the relationship between coach and team had deteriorated. Except for Tal, everyone hated Coach Sam's morale-sapping rebukes. Well aware of the tension, Tal believed that the benefits of Coach Sam's training and nutrition innovations outweighed the drawbacks. Even as disgruntlement mounted and performance times slipped, he made the decision to keep Coach Sam on for Nagano in hopes that he might work the magic of '94 again in '98.

Beginning in early 1995, Coach Sam implemented an even harder training schedule that continued into off-season training camps in Jamaica. He also took charge of developing better sleds as well as stepping up the nutrition program. The plan continued to pay dividends as the Jamaicans won a bronze medal at the World Push Championships in Monaco in September 1995, a good indicator of a team's continuing progress.

Meanwhile, Adidas recognized Coach Sam's astounding creativity and attention to detail and hired him as a paid consultant to help design the track shoes that would be worn by American sprinter Michael Johnson at the 1996 Summer Olympics. Johnson would win the gold in the 100-meter and 200-meter sprints and flash his "golden" shoes.

Also in 1995, the Jamaican Bobsleigh Federation elected Chris as the new president to replace Leo, who decided to step down and concentrate on his software marketing career. Everyone recognized that Leo's management contributions to Jamaica's advancement in the sport, particularly in 1994, could not be overstated. In order to focus on his new presidential responsibilities, Chris stepped away from bobsledding. He did, however, continue to participate in the team's training camps, as well as compete in track and field competitions that kept him fit.

As Coach Sam's saga was playing out, Devon decided to make a comeback after having sat out of the 1994 Olympics. Though his bobsled readiness had fallen off, he showed strong motivation to get back in the game. Chris appreciated Devon's renewed commitment and agreed to bring him on as a driver for the two-man sled. Tal, however, doubted that Devon had the athletic capabilities to make a good showing and would only suck more scarce training and competition funds, hurting everyone. Tal came around, though, to the idea of giving Devon a chance.

Devon did get most of his bobsledding groove back but rankled other team members by forming "Jamaica Bobsleigh Team – Harris" to raise money. The move upset the team sponsors, who saw their brand diluted.

That forced Chris to step in and temporarily suspend Devon. Nonetheless, Devon competed in enough North American circuit races to accumulate the points needed to qualify for Nagano, with Michael Morgan as his pusher/ brakeman.

Tal chose to qualify for Nagano through the more challenging A-Level World Cup circuit in Europe, which put him up against tougher European competition. Competing on this circuit, instead of the less difficult North American circuit, also held out the prospect of earning more points that could give him a higher starting position in the Olympics. Tal made it clear to the federation that if he couldn't qualify by racing against the Europeans, then he was not prepared for the Olympics.

Unfortunately, in the very first qualifying race in the two-man, another mix-up delayed the arrival of the sled to the start area. Officials were about to disqualify Tal but relented to allow him to race the heats if he started last. Since track conditions usually worsened toward the end of the races, the compromise essentially guaranteed that Tal's two-man sled would place near the bottom. That distressful beginning made it almost impossible to accumulate enough points for Olympic qualification. While Tal did not qualify for the two-man, his four-man sled placed well enough on the circuit to be within reach of securing a spot in Nagano.

Tal's long absences from home while training and competing in Europe over the years had always put a strain on Denise, who was now expecting their third child. The early, intense drive she had seen in him when they got married had manifested into a bobsled phenomena instantly recognizable around the world. She was not surprised. He had become the man he was meant to be, even as she lamented the lack of normality in their life together. Fortunately, she had family in their Kingston neighborhood for support, including Blossom, Chris's wife Michelle, Tal and Chris's sister Terry, and her own family. They were all in this together.

* * *

Between World Cup competitions in 1997, Coach Sam set up a summer training camp in Calgary for a few weeks. Tal had to travel back and forth to Jamaica and the US to keep up with the Heli Tour venture. On one of the trips back to Calgary, he brought Blossom and Denise. While showing them the track, he spontaneously asked, "Want to take a bobsled ride down with me?"

At first, they hesitated, but Tal assured them it would be fine. So the two main women in Tal's life put on a helmet, tucked into the sled, and took off. Of course, Tal did not drive as fast as he would in training or competition, but he did drive fast enough that they felt the speed and rattling. Blossom and Denise appreciated the experience but had no desire to go again.

For a few blissful days, Tal delighted in sharing a bobsled run with Blossom and Denise and getting in some good practice sessions. Soon after arriving in Florida, Tal received an anxious call from Coach Sam, who said, "Winston is trying to kill me!" Tal immediately phoned Winston and forcefully talked him out of doing anything stupid, no matter how bad he felt. At the same time Tal was speaking to Winston, he had the TV on and, in a surreal moment, saw the breaking news that Princess Diana had been killed in a car crash in Paris.

Coach Sam's berating did not subside as winter approached, and the team traveled to Winterberg for more training. Not only were team members miserable, but their mood continued to affect their load timing during practice runs. Even Tal saw that Coach Sam was hurting as much as helping but still wanted to keep him on. When Wayne made it clear that he had had enough and was ready to quit, Tal and Chris managed to persuade him to stay on in the hope that Coach Sam would fix his shortcomings.

The situation came to a head when Winston, sick of the disrespect, lunged at Coach Sam's throat and had to be pulled off by others in the room. The time had come for Coach Sam to go. Chris, as head of the Jamaican

Bobsleigh Federation, told Tal he would dismiss him, even though the coach had recently persuaded Chris to rejoin the team as a full member. But Chris held off, ever hopeful that Coach Sam would at least tone it down. One day in early December 1997, Coach Sam made disparaging remarks about Tal being stupid, an ironic statement given that Tal had been Coach Sam's only defender. Infuriated, the normally cool and unflappable Chris could take no more. He walked straight towards Coach Sam in the most intimidating manner, as if he was going to strike him. Fortunately, Wayne grabbed Chris and wrestled him to the floor. Chris fired Coach Sam on the spot.

With just six weeks to go before the Olympics, the Jamaicans were in a familiar position of having to look for a new coach, as well as a new sled. Chris reached out to his friend Trond in Norway to see if he would take the coaching job. Though excited about the prospect, Trond regretfully declined, citing other commitments he could not get out of.

While in Igls, Sepp invited the Jamaicans to dinner at his house and heard the news of Coach Sam's firing. He commented,

"Thank God!"

Sepp picked up his mobile phone and hit a speed dial button. After a short conversation in German, he turned to the team and said, "Your new coach is Gerd Leopold."

Once more, Sepp came through for the Jamaicans, this time with one of the most highly regarded coaches in the world—the one who had coached the German four-man sled to a gold medal in Lillehammer. Fortunately for the Jamaicans, the German team had shuffled their coaching staff, as they often did, leaving Gerd out and available for them. But Coach Gerd would not be able to start coaching until early January, giving him just a few weeks to get the team in top form for the Olympics that were due to commence on February 7. Until then, they were on their own as a team that had started to lose its way.

CHAPTER 36

ALMOST KNOCKED OUT

Don't focus on people trying to beat you. Instead, look inside yourself to focus on the task at hand and what you need to do. Break it all down and stitch it back together without regard to what the competition might do.

—Tal Stokes

I n late 1997, Tal was still three points short of qualifying for the Nagano Olympics in the four-man sled. A World Cup Circuit race in December in La Plagne offered the last chance to capture the remaining points. The absence of a coach until January, Chris suffering from a back injury, and having to scrounge for a sled (which they found behind a La Plagne hotel) would all make it harder. Tal had faced bigger challenges than these after ten years of racing on the World Cup circuit and three Olympics. With cool confidence, he racked up the last points. Everyone could finally relax because Jamaica officially entered the Olympics with two sleds: a four-man sled piloted by Tal and a two-man sled piloted by Devon.

After spending Christmas in Jamaica, the team returned to Igls on New Year's Day, where Coach Gerd met them with the same German four-man sled driven by Czudaj when he won the gold in Lillehammer four years earlier. As Nagano approached, it appeared things were finally looking up, especially after four years of struggle between team and coach—until they didn't.

On the first training run, Tal found the German sled a little wobbly. As he came out of turn 9, the sled flipped hard on its side and skidded all the way to the braking stretch. Everyone crawled their way out of the hull, checking on each other, as they had done after every crash. Tal, however, wandered over to sit on a bench. Chris came over to see if he was alright.

"What are you doing here?" Tal asked. "I thought you were in Idaho."

"I have not been to Idaho in years," Chris replied.

"Did you finish school?" Tal continued.

"Yes, in 1989," Chris said. "This is 1998."

It quickly became apparent that Tal had suffered a serious concussion with short-term memory loss. Normally, Tal was able to duck under the cowling to protect himself, but not in this crash. Chris began explaining to Tal what had happened over the past eleven years—that he was still married to Denise, had two lovely children, Christian and Terrie, and that Denise was pregnant with their third child to be named Michael. He told him about getting ready for Nagano and pointed out the other members of the four-man team, Wayne and Winston. When Chris mentioned that he had beaten the US team in 1994, Tal lit up with recall for a moment.

Sepp and Chris took Tal to the hospital for testing. The doctor on duty recommended that he remain for the night under observation, but that would put another dent in the team's budget. So they took Tal back to the hotel and, along with the other team members, took turns waking up Tal every hour to make sure he did not slip into a coma. Two days later, he was back in the start area, ready to drive the bobsled down for another training run. Again, he crashed and barrel-rolled the sled but managed to protect his head, as had the others. He went down the chute and crashed two more times. A sneering Austrian bobsledder labeled them "Crash Test Dummies."

That evening at the hotel, Tal called a team meeting and told them he was quitting, which also meant the four-man team would not go to the

Olympics. The team that had stuck with him through many other crashes and mishaps over the years loudly protested and refused to let him leave. For Tal, that team support marked his most cherished moment as captain of the Jamaican bobsled team.

A closer inspection of the bobsled's steering mechanism the next day revealed the reason Tal kept crashing. The "pin angle" of the bolt that controls the alignment with the runners had a looser setting than what Tal was accustomed to. Though relieved to learn that the crashes were not due to poor driving skills, Tal spent little time dwelling on his exoneration. He needed to fix the steering. Hannes Conti, a retired Austrian bobsledder, came over to see what was going on and offered to help. He and Tal worked 18 hours through the night, taking apart the sled to readjust the steering so that it worked for Tal. Once fixed, he never crashed the sled again.

After the practice runs in Igls, Coach Gerd brought the team to his impressive training gym, the Olympia, in his hometown of Reisa, once a part of East Germany. This would be the final prep before Nagano. The Jamaicans enjoyed Reisa and found the locals friendly and curious about them. Many had never seen a black person in the flesh. Coach Gerd left the four-man team line-up as it was in Lillehammer—Tal as the driver, followed by Winston, Chris, and Wayne as pushers. Michael Morgan would be the alternate. Devon and his pusher/brakeman, Jason Morris, opted not to join Tal and the rest of the four-man team in Europe with Coach Gerd. Instead, they planned to meet up in Nagano.

Coach Gerd's management style differed considerably from Coach Sam's. Every day, Coach Gerd would draw up a meticulous plan for the day and share it with the team over breakfast. He would also provide each team member with a detailed performance assessment so they knew exactly what to work on. Coach Gerd assumed that the Jamaicans had a high level of understanding about the exacting nuances of bobsledding. Coach Sam, in contrast, tended to build teams from the ground up. In that sense, he educated the sledders along the way while implementing his detailed personal research and conclusions to improve performance.

As with most German bobsled coaches, Gerd based decisions on reams of data collected by the East and West Germans for decades that could precisely pinpoint requirements. For example, the Germans had data on 1400 alloy compositions for runners and their effectiveness under every ice and temperature condition. This data could be applied with exacting precision for optimal sled performance.

For the Jamaicans, who were struggling to train and enter competitions on a meager budget, some of the million-dollar concepts Coach Gerd expounded on were well beyond their possibilities. A by-the-numbers man, Coach Gerd seldom resorted to shouting at the team, and he never demanded exercises like pushing a van up a hill the morning of a race.

At the end of the training, Coach Gerd brought the team together to share with them his expectations for the Olympics. Based on his analysis of the team's performances over the past year, he predicted the four-man team would come in 21st place, well below the laudatory 14th place they had achieved in Lillehammer. The Jamaicans sharply disagreed with Coach Gerd's assessment, claiming that, with a little more effort, they could come in 10th or even within reach of a medal. While Coach Gerd appreciated the team's enthusiasm and confidence, he quashed any higher expectations, saying, "No, no! You must be realistic. Twenty-first is a good place, and we can do this. We cannot do 10th."

The reality of comparative performance statistics clashed hard with the ambitious passion that had fueled and sustained Jamaica's unlikely quest, beginning a decade earlier. It was hard to argue with the appraisal of a world-class coach who had taken a team to a gold medal just four years earlier.

At the same time, if a coach had applied a similar analysis to the Jamaicans in 1988 after the Calgary crash and in 1992 after the disappointment of Albertville, the assessment would likely have shown that the Jamaicans had no chance of reaching the level they did at Lillehammer. Indeed, when the shoestring budget of the Jamaican bobsled program is taken into account, compared to the multi-million-dollar budgets of European teams, the achievement in Lillehammer becomes even more astonishing.

Clearly, the Jamaicans had defied the math of comparative performance, which suggested that they must have had something more going for them than merely good athletes, a modicum of training, sufficient races, and adequate sleds. After all, they beat teams with far more talent and experience in Lillehammer '94 and in World Cup races since then. What else could explain their success but the intangible factors of will, heart, and belief in themselves? If the stars lined up, a potent ambition might just compensate for wanting prowess.

One need look no further than the 1980 US Olympic hockey team beating the Soviet Union and ultimately taking the gold. Nobody doubted that the Soviet team had far more talent and experience than the collection of scrappy American "Rink Rats," but the Americans won anyhow. Still, Coach Gerd's lower but realistic expectations came as a downer for the team. The power of a dream for him was just that: a dream.

Tal and Chris, who had pursued the dream with their teammates and bucked the numbers, grasped the painful reality that Coach Gerd tried to convey. Hefty funding for sleds and training took teams to the podium. Desire alone could not replace that. The hard truth had always stared them coldly in the face without regard for zest and spirit. If Jamaica was ever going to be a serious medal contender, the team would need at least $600,000 per year over a period of six to ten years. The Jamaicans knew they would never receive more than a fraction of that.

Still, the team left Reisa amped and ready to pull off another Lillehammer in Nagano, notwithstanding Coach Gerd's disheartening prediction. Fully aware of the odds stacked against them, the Jamaicans braced themselves again to race against the best in hopes of recapturing the magic of four years earlier. Meanwhile, Devon called Tal to ask if he could use the four-man sled alternate, Michael Morgan, as the pusher/ brakeman for his two-man sled. With the extra training with the four-man team, Michael would make a better pusher than Jason. Tal, against his better judgment, agreed—a decision he would regret. The low morale that had seeped in under Coach Sam had not subsided, and tensions among team members brewed just below the surface.

CHAPTER 37

AN ERA ENDS AT NAGANO OLYMPICS '98

You need stability in your approach and stability in your execution.
You need to go into the games with everything organized and ducks in a
row. Everything that you can control, control, so you have the space to deal
with the curve balls that are going to come your way for sure.

—Tal Stokes

The IOC selection of Nagano to host the 1998 Winter Olympics came as a surprise to the two front-runners bidding for the honor, Salt Lake City and Östersund, Sweden. The balloting went down to the wire. But Nagano squeezed out a win with just a handful of votes by impressing IOC members that the city could put on the event with minimal environmental impact. By one account, Nagano spent some $14 million to entertain IOC officials inspecting the venues before selection.

The opening ceremony on February 7 began when a silver-haired farmer and lay assistant to Buddhist monks, Motoichi Godo, rang the 302-year-old bronze bell in the local temple to purify the soul. A teenager near the end of World War II, Godo had begun training to be a kamikaze pilot. Shortly before taking off on his one-way death mission, the US dropped the atomic bombs on Hiroshima and Nagasaki, and Japan surrendered days thereafter. The solemnity of Godo's befitting selection to strike the bell reverberated through the stadium as much as the deep, haunting sound itself.

Following the ringing of the bell, 72 massive sumo wrestlers entered the stadium, including the 516-lb champion Yokozuna Akebono, to perform another purification ceremony. Called *dohyo-iri*, this ceremony of thundering stomps appealed to the gods to expel evil spirits from the competition venues.

All amplified a theme of peace and harmony, even as organizers ironed out a last-minute political conflict in the marching order of nations. The normal protocol called for the nations to march into the stadium in the alphabetical order of the host country's language. The alphabetical order in the Japanese language had the contingent from Chinese Taipei (Taiwan) marching immediately after China. Both countries refused to be so close together, so the organizers switched to using English to re-establish the marching order. China followed Chile, and Taiwan followed Switzerland.

As in Lillehammer, Tal chose not to attend the opening ceremonies with his teammates so that he could focus on the race. He liked Hokkaido and meeting Japanese people, but, as always, had little interest in the Olympic pageantry. He also disdained the noisy, festive, and frivolous atmosphere of the Olympic Village. For Tal, the village, with its giant McDonald's cafeteria, resembled a fast-food all-inclusive resort that distracted from the athletic events.

Along with the bobsledders, the Jamaican delegation included Tal and Chris's sister, Terry, who found herself mobbed by fans of Jamaican bobsledding just for being their sister. The Japanese had always been avid admirers of the Jamaicans, especially after the immensely popular *Cool Runnings*. Everyone was as eager to see them in Nagano as they were in Calgary, often more interested in them than the gold medal favorites.

Inspired by the bobsled course in Lillehammer, the Nagano Olympic organizers constructed a bobsled track called "The Spiral" that also followed the contours of the slope with minimal environmental impact. That required the builders to incorporate two short, uphill sections that slowed the sled before allowing it to gain speed again on an otherwise fast course. Since Tal did not qualify in the two-man sled on the World Cup circuit, he did not have the additional practice and competition time on the track that had always given him an edge in the four-man competition.

On the first day of the two-man event on February 14, Devon and Michael Morgan placed 30th in a field of 38 after two heats. Coach Gerd reviewed with Devon how to take the curves better to increase speed, but it made little difference. The next day, Devon and Michael inched up to 29th after the final two heats.

Italy and Canada vied for the gold, with Canada 4/100ths of a second behind after the first two heats but well ahead of the traditional power-houses, Switzerland and Germany. In the third heat, Canada came within 3/100ths of a second behind Italy and managed to make up for the difference in the fourth and final run, tying Italy for the gold. The US placed 7th and 10th in the two-man, again below expectations, even after using improved Bo-Dyn sleds.

For the four-man competition set to start the following week on February 20, Jamaica had drawn number 24 for their starting position in a field of 32, a distinct disadvantage that would only get worse. Since FIBT seeded Jamaica in the bottom half of the starting order based on World Cup circuit points, the best start position they could have hoped for in the drawing would be 16th. That would have at least put them close to the top 15 group, ensuring them similar ice conditions. But luck wasn't with them despite having raced in the harder European qualifying circuit.

Unfortunately, the weather did the Nagano Olympics no favors. A warm wind from the Japan Sea, which the Japanese also called "snow eater," blew over Hokkaido. As with the Chinook wind in Calgary ten years earlier, the Japanese snow eater melted snow and ice but did not bring dust and sand. Halfway through the first heat of the four-man event, rain began to fall, causing the ice on the track to become slushy enough to slow down the sleds. By the time the Jamaicans pushed off, the ice on the track had deteriorated so badly that it left them a frustrating 21st at the end of the first heat. Rotten breaks had returned to muck up their chances.

The rain affected the ice on the track so much that officials decided to cancel the second heat altogether before it even started. The cancellation helped the top contenders, who had been among the first 15 to start, as they would not have to deal with the same slushy conditions the Jamaicans had raced through. The weather conditions did improve the next day for the third and fourth heats, but at this point, the Jamaicans had little chance of bettering their standing. After aggregating the times for just three heats (instead of the standard four, since the second heat was cancelled), Jamaica finished the event in the same 21st place, as Gerd had calculated. A late start, combined with deteriorating track conditions and a heat cancellation, factored heavily into the lower-than-expected standing.

A new generation of German and Swiss bobsledders went on to capture gold and silver, while Great Britain and France tied for bronze. The US sled driven by Shimer came in a heartbreaking 5th place, only 2/100s of a second from sharing a bronze medal (there was no fourth place because of the tie for third). In fact, the times for all the sledders were quite close together, in part because officials had decided to go with three heats instead of four.

Jamaica's 21st place hugely disappointed Tal. Watching the French and British teams take the bronze "cut through to me," Tal would later say. "Those were teams that I considered my peers and teams we had beaten on the circuit." But the French, the British, and others had resources that the Jamaicans would never have, even if the Jamaicans had as much or more talent. The other factor of warmer weather, coupled with rain, also played a key role in the standings. The warm rain was enough to overpower the refrigerated track that was supposed to keep the ice temperature the same for everyone. Had officials postponed the second heat halfway through, as they had in Calgary ten years earlier, Jamaica would surely have benefited from sliding on better ice the following day.

In the end, Tal was philosophical, as he had come to accept the fact that factors beyond his control were just part of the game. And, too often, those factors also tended to tip in favor of the top teams. Tal also understood that Jamaican bobsledding had more serious internal problems to deal with in Nagano: a breakdown in morale and escalating tensions among team members. Unlike Lillehammer '94, the Nagano four-man team was out of sync and lacked stability. The discord showed in the slower push times too, which made it impossible for a driver to make up the time lost. And then it got worse.

CHAPTER 38

DONE!

The speed and danger of bobsledding had always attracted and fostered high testosterone-fueled athletes, making them more prone to more reckless behavior than other sports. Indeed, bobsledders across all nationalities had a reputation for acting and reacting violently, even against teammates. Jamaicans were not immune to rancor that escalated into physical aggression, as had happened when Coach Sam was calling the shots. In Nagano, the antagonism exploded.

At the end of Jamaica's disappointing finish in the four-man, teammates Wayne and Michael Morgan got into a spat while the team was removing the sled runners. Michael allegedly hurled a provocative insult at Wayne. Wayne warned him to stop, but Michael spewed out another one. Wayne warned him again. At the third insult, Wayne took the runner he was holding in his hand and slammed it into Michael's chest, cracking his ribs. Wayne hit him so hard that he couldn't breathe. The team physiotherapist, who happened to be in the room, immediately began CPR chest compressions while someone else called for an ambulance. Michael survived but stayed an extra couple of days in the hospital to recover before returning home.

That was the last straw for Tal, who had given so much of his time, energy, and body to the sport, including too many concussions to count. After Lillehammer, he had little left to prove, except the possibility of making it to the podium.

The disappointing finish in Nagano for an experienced Team Jamaica, and then watching Wayne whack Michael afterwards, was not the way he wanted to go out. But few star athletes bow out on a jubilant high note of triumph with a gold medal around their necks or at the peak of their performance. More commonly, they try to get back on top, sometimes chasing the glory to savor it just one more time. Tal could have stayed in the game, as he still had the athleticism of a bobsled Olympian and had mastered the skill of steering on par with the finest drivers in the sport. As Tal himself put it, "You have to know when to pull the plug, which has always been difficult for me in whatever I've done." But the time had come. He was ready to move on.

After 10 years of bobsledding, Tal had experienced a wider world of extraordinary people and cultures. He made lifelong friends in many countries and acquired a bobsled royalty of his own. That recognition from peers was not conferred because he was the unlikely Jamaican bobsled captain from a tropical, ice-free country but because he was good, really good. Unlike the adoring public, the world-class contenders he competed against, and sometimes beat, didn't care about his color, or origin, or attitude. They saw and respected a man with a winner's drive—a bobsledder like them who had mastered their perilous and exacting sport. That's all that counted.

Tal skipped the closing ceremony and looked forward to restarting a life back in Jamaica, where Denise and his three young children waited. He had relationships to mend. Once, when returning to Jamaica from training in Europe in 1997, Tal came back to the house late at night. In a hushed voice, he announced he was home, and Denise called him to the bedroom where she was in bed with their three-year-old daughter, Terrie. As he entered the bedroom, Terrie hid behind her mother, frightened at the sight of a father she didn't recognize since he had been away so long. Over the last decade, the sport of bobsledding that had given much to Tal had taken a heavy toll as well.

PART SIX:

ONE MORE THING

CHAPTER 39

GRAND OLD MAN

To live a life that is meaningful you have to put down your ambition and take up your purpose. Both approaches may get you to the same place but the landscape around you will look very different.

—Tal Stokes

T al had cemented his reputation as the Grand Old Man of Jamaican bobsledding. His leadership and tenacity from the early days in 1987, when the whole concept of a bobsled team seemed fanciful and doomed, captured the spunk and excitement of bucking long odds. He personified the enduring myth of the reluctant hero—the one mocked and derided before rising to the occasion to pull off what no one thought was possible. Tal and the Jamaican bobsled team didn't just make their country proud in true Jamaican I-can-do-anything style but allowed all of us to root for a long shot. He let all of us believe that we too could break barriers and attain greatness. In that sense, Tal and the entire team became global role models of our time, forever woven into popular culture.

When Chris was re-elected President of the Jamaican Bobsleigh Federation in 1998, he lobbied for Jamaica to host the annual FIBT conference in Montego Bay the following year and succeeded. It was quite a coup, as the conference marked Jamaica's full acceptance into the international bobsled community as equals. The gathering of presidents of bobsled federations from around the world on a tropical island also signified that bobsledding had become a winter sport without climate boundaries.

The President of the FIBT, Bob Storey, was not about to let the moment pass without honoring the man most responsible for bobsledding's transition from the realm of a clubby few to a global phenomena. In fact, the sport had evolved well beyond an eclectic collection of daredevils careening down an ice track to become an unexpected metaphor for anyone, anywhere, reaching for the stars. With that in mind, Storey presented Tal with the President's Trophy, the highest honor conferred by bobsledding's international governing body. In his presentation remarks, Storey said that Tal is one of those rare athletes who "gives more to the sport than he takes away." In 2000, the Jamaican government followed up by honoring Tal with the Order of Distinction, Officer Class, one of the country's highest awards.

Though Tal had never sought the spotlight, he deeply appreciated the accolades bestowed upon him. Distressingly, the honors did little to fix his more pressing problem: He was nearly broke. A decade in pursuit of becoming a world-class bobsledder had seriously constrained him from making money, much less accumulating any savings. In fact, he was saddled with debt. One hundred thousand dollars of debt was not unusual for many Olympic athletes. It was part of the price tag for a shot at glory even against hopelessly long odds.

Tal's helicopter business with Will initially contributed some income to his growing household but barely. But the unceasing strife in Jamaica, followed by declining tourism, hit the business hard. And when terrorists attacked the US on 9/11, international travel almost dried up completely, and business fell off to the point where Heli-Tours had to close.

Through all the years of Tal's bobsledding, Denise had covered much of his expenses while he competed abroad, as well as cared for the family. She understood and accepted her husband's singular journey to be a top bobsled driver because that's who he was as a man. But to say that Denise emphatically supported his quest that took him away from home for months at a time, year after year, would be an exaggeration. She stood strong by her driven man but also forged her own identity as a mother and a woman juggling a household and managing a business.

Denise worked for a shipping brokerage company in Kingston in the late 1990s and was tasked with signing on clients and handling their import and export requirements. Profits rose significantly. After a year on the job, she asked for a share of the company. The owners said, "No," so Denise quit and started her own third-party logistics company and took the clients she had acquired with her. She called her company Aeromour and quickly established herself in the industry. Aeromour did well, and both Denise and Tal saw the potential for expanding the revenue if Tal jumped in full time and applied his logistics experience.

As Tal turned to making a living and paying off personal debts, Chris worked hard to bring in more resources to keep the Jamaican bobsled team's momentum going. He recruited his Norwegian friend, Trond, to be the national coach for both the men's and women's teams. Already familiar with the Jamaican program and local talent, Trond needed little orientation and set about recruiting and training the best athletes he could find.

While Jamaica had qualified for each of the Olympics from 1988 through 1998, there was no assurance that Jamaica would qualify for the 2002 Winter Olympics in Salt Lake City or any future Olympics. Qualifying would always be a struggle, with more demanding requirements to accumulate points for limited spots. At the same time, the well-funded European teams, along with the US and Canadian teams, continued to grow stronger.

Neither Chris nor Trond nor the up-and-coming Jamaican bobsledders were about to let Tal recede to the sidelines. They all regularly tapped into his formidable expertise to advise and mentor the new generation of sledders. In preparation for the 2002 Winter Olympics, the new male and female bobsledders—women would start competing for the first time in the Salt Lake City Games—insisted that he practice with them on the new track located in Park City, Utah, where the bobsled competition would be held. Tal obliged and piloted the sled down the chute with the newbies and shared the critical skills that he had learned over the years.

Despite the tougher road to securing an Olympic spot, Jamaica qualified for the Salt Lake City Games in the two-man sled. Piloted by Winston Watts (who had switched from pusher), with Lascelles Brown as pusher/brakeman, the team finished a credible 28th out of 38 entries. The American sled, driven by Todd Hays, finished just off the podium in an agonizing fourth place, only 3/100ths of a second from bronze.

In the two-woman race, a first at the Winter Olympics, the US team, driven by Jill Bakken, won gold. Hays saw redemption by winning silver as the pilot for the four-man sled. The Team USA II four-man sled, piloted by Brian Shimer, also made the podium with a bronze. Together, the Americans, women and men, finally ended the 46-year medal drought driving Bo-Dyn sleds.

Distressingly, the Jamaicans did not qualify for the Winter Olympic Games in Torino in 2006 or Vancouver in 2010. However, they made a comeback in the 2014 Winter Olympics held in Sochi, Russia, in the two-man sled, with veteran Winston Watts as the pilot at the age of 46 and Marvin Dixon as the pusher/brakeman. They placed 27th out of 30. Perennial lack of funding almost kept them from going to Sochi at all, but the cryptocurrency Dogecoin community raised $30,000 of the $40,000 needed just in time.

After the 2014 Winter Games, Chris persuaded 2002 silver medalist Hays, now retired from competition, to coach the team. Bringing on a top racer like Hays was a great boost to the Jamaican program. But the federation, predictably, ran short of money and could not retain him past one season. Hays continued, however, to be an informal advisor without pay.

Around the same time, a half a world away in Japan, the development of a new sled would force a reckoning with Jamaican bobsledding's identity: Would the Jamaicans be the delightfully dogged crowd-pleasers, as portrayed in *Cool Runnings*? Or were they in it to be world-class sledders on a global stage, as happened in Lillehammer '94?

* * *

In the first decade of the new Millennium, Tal and Denise built their 3PL custom brokerage agency into an impressive multi-million-dollar enterprise. While the gross revenue was high, the profit margins were thin, and some of their bigger business clients delayed payment for services or neglected to pay at all because they could. Fighting the powerful companies in court was simply unaffordable. The frequent cash crunches they faced constantly strained the business and them.

At the same time, the violence in Jamaica had not abated. Although Tal, Denise, and their family were largely shielded because they lived in a nicer Kingston neighborhood, their employees were not so fortunate. Three of them were shot dead in one year, and one was badly wounded. All good people. Two had been lifelong friends of the family and spent much time living in their home.

In 2012, when the children were in their late teens, Tal and Denise decided that the troubles and heartbreak in Jamaica were too much. They decided to pull up stakes and move to Providenciales ("Provo") in the Turks and Caicos Islands, where Tal had citizenship because of his birth in the country. Provo had emerged as a high-end tourist destination. With miles and miles of stunning white-sand beaches that spilled into the mesmerizing turquoise waters of Grace Bay, Provo presented an inviting contrast to the congested, edgy city of Kingston. Here they could begin anew. And with only an hour and a half of flying time to Jamaica, Tal and Denise could easily return to see family, and he could mentor up-and-coming bobsledders.

For Tal, life had come full circle back to the islands where his parents had first arrived as Baptist missionaries more than a half century earlier. But the murder of friends and the anguish of losing the business, as well as some misgivings over his harsh leadership style and long absences from the family, gnawed at him. Being introspective by nature, Tal started writing a book as therapy to climb out of a dark space. He laid out his accumulated wisdom and regrets over the course of his adult life, especially the years learning the art and science of bobsledding. As usual, he didn't hold back and named the book *Advice I should have taken: (And other things I think I have learnt)*. The reflective writing seemed to work, as the perspective of time and distance imbued him with a greater clarity of purpose.

After some prodding, Tal became an occasional public speaker, recounting the adventures of the legendary Jamaican Bobsled Team while also imparting insights into business management. Once on stage, he proved to have the same charisma as his father. Cruise ships, corporate boards of directors, and CEOs hired him to share his compelling stories. At first Tal felt surprised that audiences were excited to hear his anecdotes about the Jamaican bobsledders and lessons he had learned. But the lessons over time were not all joyful or about finding inner peace or universal love, the usual uplifting messages by famous athletes who had turned speakers. Yes, there is the grand story arc of rising from humble island beginnings and closing with fame and self discovery. But for Tal the journey was as much about accepting disappointment and disillusion tempered by sporadic moments of happiness and, on rare occasion, ecstasy. He had a more profound message to convey—a raw, unsentimental and sober take on the world—clear-eyed but not dire.

"The first and most significant change for me took place between 1988 and 1994, when I was learning the basics of bobsleighing because that is when I learned the need to confront reality in a fairly ruthless way without any window dressing or sweeteners to make it more palatable. I had to set aside a belief that things would be all right or that somebody else would come along to help me. You as the individual bore all responsibility. You alone have to make realistic assessments and to make sure you prepare yourself throughly for what's before you. That's the main thing, and that stayed with me down through the years."

Tal's bobsledding career opened his eyes to the underbelly of the sport that contrasted sharply with the world of politicians, renowned athletes, and the generally well-off who were instrumental in advancing bobsledding in Jamaica and worldwide. The overlooked and invisible underclass proved to be just as crucial to his achievement even if quite different from him.

"Bobsleighing exposed me to a side of Europe that many people don't know. And I should also add America and Canada to this because bobsleigh runs are largely in rural, mountainous areas where ordinary people lived, away from glitzy ski resorts. In these places, whether in the Alps of Germany, Austria, Switzerland, France, Italy, or the Rocky Mountain foothills outside Calgary, or the Adirondacks of upstate New York, you spend your time with truck drivers and snow plowers and track workers. People working with their hands and on machines. In the course of bobsleighing, you get to know the backbone of these places. You see a different side of a country, the bread and butter people who are not well-known."

These were also the people who also made up most of the bobsledders who were training and competing. Their tough and hardened backgrounds, those whose paychecks didn't always cover the expenses, left little room for the popular life-broadening experiences of the middle and upper classes. Driving or pushing a bobsled faster than anyone else for a chance, however slim, to stand on the podium while risking almost certain injury over and over was one of the few tickets out—an out that few would ever see. They too suffered and struggled, but the bobsled gave them a sense of purpose and status in the community, and the smallest of hope. The hidden subculture of gritty lives on the lower end, too often marked by dead-ends and despair regardless of country, pounded into Tal a profound respect. They were the ones who got the bobsled fixed and the track ready for competition that made his success and the success of others possible. And he learned from them a fortitude to keep going despite them having few prospects for breaking away.

Initially, Tal didn't give much thought to the possibility that his journey from a JDF helicopter pilot to international role model as the captain of the Jamaican bobsled team might actually earn him a post-bobsled career income or draw an audience wanting to hear him. He never saw himself as a motivational speaker, but over time his talks resonated with multiple generations, even 30 years after Calgary, and packed the rooms. And he soon found that he had much to give back with his own brand of inspiration based on how he had changed that went beyond from the popular feel-good narratives of self-discovery. More than anything, he wanted to not just raise awareness of a barely visible underclass but bring them front and center because they make possible the ambitions for the rest of us.

On one occasion, Tal's newfound ability to inspire almost brought him to tears. After he had given a presentation on a cruise ship sailing through the Caribbean, a mother and a father brought their teenage son confined to a wheelchair to meet him. It turned out that just before leaving on the cruise, the boy had brought with him a CD of Cool Runnings that he enthusiastically played over and over. The boy's unexpected chance encounter with the real Jamaican bobsled captain on the cruise turned out to be one of those unforgettable life experiences for the boy and for Tal.

In Provo, Tal continued to stay in terrific shape and often walked around his neighborhood carrying big water jugs filled with small rocks to maintain muscle tone. He never stopped feeding his body with high-end nutrients to maintain optimal brain health and stayed current on the science of concussions. Despite being a true celebrity, he kept a low profile in the Turks & Caicos, attending few parties, and choosing friends carefully. Denise, more outgoing and social, quickly established herself as a go-to person on the island for boat charters and logistical support that progressed to luxury villa management. The singular story of the Jamaican Bobsled Captain should have ended here, as Tal passed through middle age with the status of a revered village elder in Jamaica and on a global stage. A more interesting and successful life on which to rest one's laurels would be hard to match. At last, he had found some contentment. But the gods of bobsledding, as well as the demons, were not about to let Tal slide quietly into the night. He had one more mission for the soul of Jamaican bobsledding.

CHAPTER 40

SHITAMACHI SHOWDOWN

The Japanese refer to the old, traditional communities of Tokyo as the *Shitamachi*. The literal translation approximates "lower city" that is geographically closer to the river and sea as well as being flood-prone. But a more nuanced meaning refers to a lower class section of Tokyo with narrow alleys and low buildings—an area that contrasts with the hilly, more affluent part of of the city. Indeed, for hundreds of years, the Shitamachi has been the home of commoners and the small entrepreneurs, skilled craftsmen, artists, and small manufacturers.

In early 1945, the US Air Force had become frustrated that its B-29 bombers had only limited success in knocking out scattered Japanese factories. General Curtis LeMay, who took charge of the bombing campaign, decided to change tactics and use incendiary bombs to burn the residential areas of Tokyo and other cities. Some of the young American pilots, mostly in their early to mid-20s, at first declined to fly the missions because they did not want to kill civilians. Senior officers pressured them into it, however, by rationalizing that they would be bombing factory workers supporting the war effort, and this would end the war sooner.

The raids began on March 10, 1945, and burned to death 100,000 people in Tokyo alone, including those living in the Shitamachi districts. The bombers flew low enough so that smoke from the fires enveloped and seeped into the planes and carried the stench of burning flesh. Decades later, surviving air crews, interviewed by the *New York Times*, recalled the horror of those raids and their deep regrets about what they had done.

In the years following World War II, the Shitamachi recovered and soon became a hub of Japanese industrial manufacturing, with small-scale subcontractors producing high-tech components for cars, bullet trains, and aircraft. The rebuilt Shitamachi continued to display a more friendly, humbler side of Tokyo, set apart from the gleaming skyscrapers of the real downtown, filled with eager "salarymen" frantically climbing the corporate ladder of "Japan Inc." The Ota ward, one of the Shitamachi communities hardest hit by the incendiary bombs, at one point boasted more than 9,000 factories, 80% of which employed fewer than 10 workers. While the small and medium entrepreneurs maintained a reputation for stellar craftsmanship, the high-status mega-corporations tended to look down on them as low-status. Shitamachi residents felt and resented that slight.

In 2012, factory owner Satoshi Kosugi decided that the Ota ward was long overdue for recognition as a world-class tech center on par with the dominant corporate powers of Japan. He hit on the idea of building the best bobsled on the planet as a way to make a splash in a thrilling event and show off the district's advanced industrial prowess. He broached the idea to Jun'ichi Hosogai, who owned an aluminum processing factory in Ota. Hosogai also saw the potential for a Japanese-made bobsled at the Olympics to reap publicity and took charge.

The Japanese public had little interest in bobsledding, and nobody in the Ota ward had ever built a bobsled. Nonetheless, Kosugi and Hosogai maintained confidence that Ota's technical talent was up to the task and wanted to go big. They persuaded 40 small factories in Ota to commit to a collective effort in what became known as "The Shitamachi Bobsleigh Project" (referred to as the "Shitamachi Project"). The Ota ward also had a powerful political ally on their side with then Prime Minister Shinzo Abe, who was also a personal friend of Hosogai.

The Shitamachi Project disassembled a borrowed German bobsled to its basic components and invited the Ota entrepreneurs to claim pieces, such as bolts, axels, runners, and cowling, to manufacture at higher standards. In less than a month, they produced a new bobsled and offered it to Japanese bobsled teams. Prime Minister Abe was so taken with the idea of Japanese-produced bobsleds that he singled out the effort in a policy speech to the Japanese Diet (Parliament), similar to the US President's State of the Union address.

The sled had limited success in Japanese competition, however, and when the 2014 Sochi Olympics came along, the Japanese national team decided to go with another foreign sled. Disappointed by the Japanese team's surprising rejection but undeterred, Hosogai approached Chris, as he was the president of the Jamaica Bobsleigh Federation. Hosogai offered to provide free sleds for the Jamaican teams, as well as sled transportation. Working with the Jamaicans seemed to be a good match since *Cool Runnings* had been wildly popular in Japan. Indeed, the movie had made Jamaicans super-cool folk heroes—the little guys who made it to the big times through spunk and pluck. The Shitamachi communities, in particular, could relate to the movie's portrayal of Jamaican bobsled underdogs going up against sneering, dismissive competitors. Building the actual sled the Jamaicans would use in Olympic competition could only amplify that connection and finally allow Shitamachi to break out of the Japan Inc. shadow.

For cash-strapped Team Jamaica, the Shitamachi sled was an offer they could not pass up. Good used sleds then cost around $40,000. In 2016, the Jamaican Bobsleigh Federation signed a contract with The Shitamachi Project to use their sleds for qualifying matches on their path to the 2018 Olympics in Pyeongchang, South Korea, and at the Games themselves, if they made it. Both sides celebrated the win-win agreement until the doubts about the sled trickled in.

* * *

While practicing on the Shitamachi sled at the Calgary track in early 2017, Jamaica's star female pilot in the two-woman sled, American-born Jazmine Fenlator-Victorian, told Chris the sled rattled too much and gave her headaches. Worse, she felt unsafe. She admired the quality of the components, but the sled felt too stiff. More precisely, it showed none of the flexibility needed when entering and exiting turns. Since a bobsled has no shock absorbers, it has to dampen the vibrations with a suspension that allows it to "bend" or "articulate" as it winds through the chute. Without such flexibility, the sled vibrates too much and slides slower.

Jazmine had plenty of bobsledding experience and knew her sleds. A top track and field athlete from New Jersey, she switched to bobsledding after college and raced for the US Olympic bobsled team in the 2014 Sochi Games, placing 11th. After Sochi, she decided to compete for Jamaica since she was able to claim Jamaican citizenship through her father's heritage. Jazmine had a good shot at qualifying for the 2018 Olympics and representing Jamaica on its first women's Olympic bobsled team, but only if she had a good sled.

Chris became increasingly concerned that the federation may very well have found itself stuck with a questionable piece of equipment. Continued use of the sled risked injury to the Jamaican bobsledders and could hamper even qualifying for the 2018 Olympics. Chris called Todd Hays and asked if he would fly to Tokyo to meet with Shitamachi Project managers and engineers to evaluate the sled's production at the site in Ota.

Hays agreed. He had all the experience and technical credentials one could ask for. In addition to being a silver medalist in the 2002 Salt Lake City Games, he had been involved in the Bo-Dyn project and built his own sled that won the 2012 World Championship. More recently, Hays had been the US tech lead for the BMW bobsled project that won three medals for the US in the 2014 Sochi Games. He had already coached the Jamaican team and started coaching the Canadian bobsled team. The Canada Bobsleigh Federation didn't mind lending him out, as they supported helping less affluent countries develop competitive bobsled programs. Hays brought with him another bobsled engineer, Oliver Brower.

The Shitamachi Project management and engineers warmly welcomed Hays and Brower when they arrived in Tokyo. It was not the first trip to the city for Hays, however. In 1995, a fight promoter invited Hays, the US kickboxing champion at the time, to Tokyo to fight Japan's undefeated ultimate-fighting champion, Koichiro Kimura. Hays beat him in front of 60,000 screaming Japanese fans. Nobody at Shitamachi held the painful defeat of their home-boy star against him, however. They respected Hays's expertise and outstanding bobsled career.[1]

The superb Japanese craftsmanship of each component of the Shitamachi bobsled impressed Hays and Brower. As excellent as the quality was for each piece of the sled, it didn't work when assembled. In particular, Hays noted that the carbon-fiber-reinforced plastic frame felt stiff, as Jazmine had complained about. The engineers had apparently applied multiple coatings of resin over Kevlar cloth and "baked" it all in an oven to create a bullet-proof frame second-to-none. In the process, however, they eliminated any "give." Hays recommended interspersing the resin layers with foam or honeycomb to allow the sled flexibility, along with some other fixes. The Shitamachi Project people vaguely indicated that they might consider some changes.

Hays wondered if something was lost in translation through the interpreters, who maybe didn't communicate his suggestions precisely. Or perhaps the Shitamachi Project engineers simply didn't think they needed any advice as their craftsmanship was so plainly superior. In any case, after a week, Hays and Brower returned home disappointed, though not entirely surprised. High-profile car companies, including Ferrari and McLaren, as well as other reputable tech manufacturers, had tried to engineer their way to build a better bobsled. Almost all failed. The only successful bobsleds

---

1 When Hays returned to Texas after the match, he watched a demo-push by bobsledders touring the US to encourage athletes from other sports to try bobsledding. Todd decided this was going to be his sport and invested the money he won kickboxing in Japan to become a bobsledder.

were built by FES, BTC, Bo-Dyn, and BMW. Their sleds won races because actual bobsledders worked side by side with engineers from start to finish with equal status.

*   *   *

As the fall of 2017 approached and bobsled season resumed, nothing had been resolved with the Shitamachi sled. Jazmine tried the sled on the Park City track but continued to grumble about its performance. Chris called Tal to ask if he would fly up and check out the sled as well as help coach Jazmine through two qualifying races coming up in December in Germany and Austria.

In Park City, Tal examined the Shitamachi sled and completely agreed with Hays, Brower, and Jazmine's assessment about stiffness and a number of other problems and confirmed Chris's reservations. They decided that Jazmine would not use the Shitamachi sled anymore for training or races until the problems were fixed.

Around the same time, Chris and Leo hired Sandra Kiriasis from Germany to be Jazmine's new driver coach. Sandra was one of the most decorated bobsledders of all time, with World Championships and Olympic gold and silver medals to her credit. Jazmine had competed against Sandra and knew her well. It seemed like a good fit, especially when Sandra offered to help obtain a BTC bobsled from her bobsled club in Germany for Jazmine to drive. The BTC sled was actually made in Latvia with engineering advice from Hays and was widely considered the second fastest sled in the world at the time, after the German FES sleds. However, the Germans did not let anyone else drive the technically superior FES.

At the qualifying races in Winterberg and Igls, Jazmine and her pusher/brakewoman, Carrie Russell, performed well in both competitions racing in the BTC and began accumulating Olympic qualifying points. At the same time, the Shitamachi Project leaders kept reminding the Jamaicans about the contract they had signed. They minced no words in making clear their insistence, "You must use the Shitamachi sled."

A team of Shitamachi Project junior managers and mechanics flew to Austria to meet with Tal and show off their "improved" sled. Tal checked it over and remained unconvinced. He was not going to take a chance on Jazmine failing to qualify by using a problematic sled, even with modifications, or risking injuries.

Tal returned to Provo for Christmas, thinking that his work was done. But Chris asked him to return to Europe in January to keep working with Jazmine and Carrie through two more competitive qualifying races in Altenberg and Königsee, Germany, before a final race in St. Moritz. At this point, only the Jamaican women had a realistic chance, though far from assured, of securing a spot for the 2018 Olympics.

Soon after the Jamaicans arrived at Königsee for the second race, they were met by Hosogai himself. With the reputation of the Ota ward and the Shitamachi sled on the line, the Japanese concept of *meiyo*, meaning "honor," became preeminent. Hosogai was determined to hold Jamaica to their contract. Meanwhile, Hosogai kept his good friend, Prime Minister Abe, informed and engaged. The Shitamachi Project had gone all-in, and Hosogai was not about to let their showcase sled be dismissed by Jamaican bobsledders, especially given Jamaica's popularity in Japan.

The Japanese embassy in Kingston contacted Chris directly to urge him to reconsider and use the Shitamachi sled instead of BTC. Chris declined. Unexpectedly caught in the middle was Jamaica's ambassador to Japan, Ricardo "Ricky" Allicock. He quickly picked up on the growing tension and offered to help find an acceptable resolution for all parties. He had seen first-hand Japanese admiration for Jamaica and Jamaican bobsledders in particular. Once, the Jamaican embassy in Tokyo had received through the mail an unregistered letter from Okinawa with one million yen ($9,300) in cash. A note tucked in with the cash requested that the money be given to the Jamaican bobsled program.

The Jamaican Ministry of Foreign Affairs back in Kingston was quite cognizant of the Japanese goodwill toward Jamaica and intent on maintaining that positive "J to J" relationship that had been cultivated over decades. Indeed, that relationship was regularly reinforced when representatives from the two countries sat next to each other at international conferences because of the alphabetic order of the names. Ambassador Allicock kept his ministry informed of the Shitamachi Project's steadfast expectation that the Jamaican Bobsleigh Federation would use their sled despite Jamaican resistance. At the same time, the Japanese Ministry of Foreign Affairs had been tracking the Shitamachi Project's mounting confrontation with the Jamaican bobsledders, as had Prime Minister Abe's office.

Leo set up Zoom meetings to connect him and Chris with Tal in Germany, as well as Ambassador Allicock in Tokyo, to figure out how to deal with the Shitamachi Project's full-court press. Coincidentally, Ambassador Allicock had been childhood friends with Tal and Chris and was keen to resolve the impasse with an amicable solution. Between Zoom meetings, Tal and Hosogai negotiated for ten hours through the night and into the early morning in an effort to break the stalemate. But Tal wouldn't budge. He threw out a bone by suggesting that maybe the BTC sled could be rebranded as a Shitamachi sled if that would make them feel better. The Shitamachi managers balked at the notion.

After more discussions, the Shitamachi Project leadership partially relented to let the Jamaican women continue to use the BTC sled for the two remaining qualifying races in January. At the Olympics, however, the Japanese expected the Jamaicans to switch to the Shitamachi sled after they made some additional adjustments. Tal didn't believe for a minute that the Shitamachi Project engineers would ever be able to make the sled worthy of racing in anyone's lifetime.

Still, the whole dispute over a contractual obligation had dramatically escalated into the dreadful prospect of *haji,* meaning "shame or embarrassment."

CHAPTER 41

JAMAICANS STAND FIRM

J ust before the Olympics, the Shitamachi Project arranged to have the Japanese low-budget airline, Skymark, paint the fuselage of one of their planes with a Shitamachi bobsled. To underscore their unshakable confidence that the Jamaicans would be using the sled in Pyeongchang, they even had the bobsled painted in the green, black, and yellow colors of the Jamaican flag.

At the last qualifying race in St. Moritz, Jazmine earned an Olympic spot in the two-woman bobsled by just one point. She and Carrie, with Audra Segree as an alternate, would be Jamaica's only bobsled team at the Olympics. By this time, Chris, Tal, and Leo had arranged for the BTC sled to be shipped to Pyeongchang as Jamaica's Olympic sled. Jamaica's Minister of Sports, Olivia "Babsy" Grange, backed the decision. She stated to Chris, "Do what you believe is best for Jamaica."

*   *   *

Tal still believed he could slip back into his quiet Turks and Caicos home, far from the madding crowd, but not yet. The stand-off with Shitamachi remained. At the same time, Tal and others on the coaching/management staff had mounting doubts about Coach Sandra's capabilities. Although she had proven to be the best bobsledder in the world, her racing success, they believed, had not carried over to team building or the technical skills required in a coach. To help contain a potential double crisis, Chris brought Tal back to be part of the Jamaican Olympic delegation in Pyeongchang.

Audra carried the Jamaican flag in the opening ceremonies at Pyeongchang, followed by teammates Jazmine and Carrie, Chris, Leo, Coach Sandra, and Jamaica's skeleton sled racer, Anthony Watson. But the delegation didn't just staidly walk into the stadium and wave to the spectators like everyone else. Rather, they broke into a reggae dance that lit up the internet, easily making them the crowd favorite. Not even the cross-country skier and flag bearer from Tonga, Pita Taufatofua, could match the Jamaicans despite showing off his oiled and glistening bare chest while marching in the freezing cold. As in almost all modern Olympics, the organizers highlighted themes of peace and harmony. South Korea personified that by having the delegation from North Korea march with them as a unified team amid dazzling displays of fire and fireworks. Also sitting in the stands with other national leaders was Japan's Prime Minister Abe.

The two-woman bobsled race was set for mid-week, February 20 and 21. The training runs in the BTC sled the week before had gone well for Jazmine and Carrie, and they even placed ninth in one of them. They named their BTC sled "Mr. Cool Bolt" in honor of sprinter Usain Bolt, who had won eight Olympic gold medals for Jamaica. Before the week ended, however, Chris, Leo, Tal, and the other coaches had lost all confidence in Coach Sandra. Chris moved her from head coach to track performance analyst, a clear demotion. Coach Sandra quit and made a series of media appearances to complain publicly about her treatment, stating, "I have never known such disappointment in this sport in my life." Chris responded to the press by saying, "Sandra Kiriasis was a hugely destructive force on the team. Now that she is off the team, the synergy is much better."

Upset at what she considered unfair treatment, Coach Sandra took back the BTC sled, claiming she was responsible for it. As the explosive rift that threatened to derail Jamaica's participation in the Olympics received extensive play in the media, Tal stepped in to be the head coach for a team without a sled and whose Olympic dream was fading quickly.

Meanwhile, senior Shitamachi Project officials had already shipped their still-work-in-progress Shitamachi sled to Pyeongchang, while they flew in on a private jet. Loss of face and national humiliation loomed large, as they still had not been able to convince the Jamaicans to switch sleds. As soon as the Shitamachi Project people heard that Coach Sandra had taken away the BTC sled, they jumped into the fray. Circumstances and serendipity, it seemed, had suddenly opened the door for the Jamaicans to finally go with the Shitamachi sled since, at this point, they had no choice.

*   *   *

On the other side of the world, in Kingston, the Jamaican bobsled team's reliable sponsor, Red Stripe, closely watched the distressing turn of events unfold. Mindful of Team Jamaica's preference for the BTC sled, Red Stripe officials contacted Chris and Leo. "What would it take," Red Stripe asked, "to buy the BTC sled for Jazmine and Carrie to race in?" Leo called Sandra's club in Germany and found out that the Jamaican Bobsleigh Federation could purchase the same BTC sled on the spot for $40,000. Without hesitation, Red Stripe said, "Do it! We got you covered." Tal and the team took possession of the sled just in time for Jazmine and Carrie to race.

But possession was not quite enough. When IOC officials learned that a Red Stripe donation had been used to purchase the BTC sled, they expressed concern that it might violate IOC rules against unauthorized sponsorship at an Olympic event. Quick behind-the-scenes phone calls and meetings, in the spirit of George Fitch's wheeling and dealing 30 years earlier, convinced the IOC to let it go.

Jazmine and Carrie finished the first three heats in 18th, 16th, and 18th place for each heat. The less-than-stellar performance appeared odd since Jazmine and Carrie had placed much better on the World Cup circuit and in the Olympic practice runs. In the third heat, Tal noticed sparks occasionally flying out from the runners when the sled banked on the turns. He brought the team mechanic over to inspect the sled, and they determined that the brake's "tooth-bar" was loose and scraped against the ice when the force of gravity was strongest on the curves. A loose tooth-bar does happen on rare occasions when the brake lever, located between the brake person's knees, malfunctions and drops down during the run. But it is difficult for the brake person to notice since the brake still functions to stop the sled after the finish. The mechanic fixed the brake, and Jazmine and Carrie finished 13th in the fourth and final heat, thus showing they were capable of far better times. Unfortunately, it was not enough to pull them out of the bottom, and they finished in 18th place out of 20.

Shitamachi officials had been so confident that the Jamaicans would use their sled that they hired a videographer to record the entire initiative for a documentary. The original intent was to highlight the success of the Shitamachi-Jamaican bobsled cooperation. After being rebuffed, Shitamachi officials were devastated. They turned the video documentary into a swipe of the once-lovable Jamaican bobsledders with the Japanese as victims. A heartbroken Ambassador Allicock watched Japanese national television portray Jamaica in a terrible light. Despite the negative documentary, however, many Japanese thought that the Shitamachi project had overreached in its ambition and set themselves up for failure and *haji*. Japanese society was quite open to considering differing points of view, even when one of their own took a hit.

All along, Tal, Chris, and Leo had stood firm when it counted. They decisively chose to give the Jamaican athletes the best sled and the best chance to perform as far as their talents would take them. They pushed back on the pressure to race a sled that was not ready for prime time. In doing so, they signaled that Jamaica had embraced the sport as a contender, not to promote someone else's agenda. Jamaicans raced for national pride and a place on the podium. Whatever the cost, bobsledding belonged to them as much as any other country.

EPILOGUE

After the Olympics in Pyeongchang, the Jamaica Bobsleigh Federation re-elected Chris as president for the fourth time. The Shitamachi sled quarrel and the coach drama at Pyeongchang, as well as years of struggle, convinced him to revamp the entire approach to bobsledding and lay out a plan. First, draw deeply from the well of talented Jamaicans everywhere in the country, not just who shows up. Second, identify prospective bobsled athletes in their teens and bring them up through the ranks more like the Europeans. Third, partner with Lake Placid to make the Mt. Van Hoevenberg track the official Jamaican Bobsled Training Center and send the bobsledders there to get as much training as the powerhouse teams.

Funding for the Jamaican Bobsleigh Federation will always be a challenge, especially to acquire fast, high-end sleds. But that challenge could be alleviated by standardizing two and four-person sleds. The international federation, now called the International Bobsleigh & Skeleton Federation (IBSF), had already done that for the new monobobs (one-person sleds approved for women's events). In fact, most national bobsled federations want to standardize sleds to level the playing field and diminish the power of money as a factor in standing on the podium. The Germans are the main holdouts, as they continue to have the advantage with technologically superior sleds, thanks to multimillion-dollar funding, including hefty government subsidies. With or without standardized sleds, however, the Jamaican Bobsleigh Federation's goal will always be to train teams using great sleds that can beat the best.

* * *

When the pandemic hit and brought economic and social life to a screeching halt in 2020, Tal and Denise's adult children, then in their early twenties and living in Great Britain, decided to set up a streaming of *Cool Runnings* for all their friends. But with a twist. They asked their dad to provide a running commentary about how the film did and did not compare to the real story. It was the perfect antidote to the grim lockdown, and the kids loved the movie.

The special streaming was the first time that Tal had seen the movie since its debut in 1993. With 27 years of perspective, he gained a new and grudging appreciation for what Dawn Steel and Hollywood were trying to do—have a little fun telling a story that everyone could relate to. He recognized that the film had stood the test of time by connecting with audiences over three generations. Tal's critical perspective provided a rare and entertaining moment where the two universes of movie fantasy and harsh reality merged, if only for a couple of hours.

Hollywood's version of events tends to bend toward fiction, not fact, which in turn forms public perceptions that can be far removed from truth. History, too, tends to be re-imagined after a couple of generations with simpler and more relatable narratives of noble conquests or fight-to-the-death heroes, often to suit the personal or national agenda of those in power. In doing so, the more complex and uncomfortable truth of what actually happened to real people gets lost. It is a tendency we should not easily accept.

Allowing uncomplicated narratives of reality to take hold, even if inspiring and uplifting, deflects and detracts from the pain and agonizing setbacks the players endured along the way. If we neglect the struggle and suffering they pushed through, we lose pieces of their lives to the past and diminish our own. After all, what forged those who came before has shaped us today and will mold those who follow.

The full and unsparing story of strong, determined, and sometimes flawed men bound by a seemingly unattainable goal illuminates and validates that most human of desires: to discover how far we can go, even when everyone says we can't. The honest revelations of those who stepped into the unknown embolden the rest of us, with our own qualms, to find our path as fellow travelers on an unbroken journey of human exploration.

One hundred years from now, long after our bones are interred, the unique yet universal tale of the first Jamaican bobsled team and its captain, Dudley "Tal" Stokes, will be told, retold, and likely spun with the passage of time. In what will surely be a different era, fraught with its own tribulations, their essential story will be there to spur on those who choose the untrodden track with all its peril. That wholly improbable convergence of eclectic visionaries, early believers, demanding coaches, supportive families, and uncommon athletes, battered, bruised, and unbowed, did something extraordinary with their lives and their time on this earth: They defied the naysayers of their day and told us we could do the same. Generations to come will hear them whisper: *Dismiss the doubters, cope with crashes, and stay the course, for you are not alone.*

The End

AFTERWORD

Tal and Denise Stokes continue to live on Providenciales, well integrated into the island community. Tal maintains close contact with friends he has made from all over the world and has not let up on his writing or commentaries. In addition to his blogs and podcast, *TalStokes360*, he completed an audiobook, *Ready Everyday*, which delves into the science and practical applications of achieving peak performance anytime, anywhere. Cruise ships and corporate groups regularly book him as a motivational speaker. Denise maintains her own fierce cardio and strength-building workout routine before starting the day as manager for some of the most luxurious villas on the island. Tal and Denise treasure time with their children and with Tal's mother, Blossom, who flies over from Jamaica a couple of times a year.

Chris Stokes continues to chair the Jamaica Bobsleigh Federation and energetically uses his influence and accumulated knowledge to recruit and train new bobsledders who can take on the world. He received a Ph.D. in Economic Development Policy from the University of the West Indies and, after holding senior management positions in Jamaican financial institutions, founded his own financial management company, NCS Financial Services Group. He provides high-end economic development services for the public and private sectors in Jamaica and the Caribbean. The Jamaican government awarded Chris the *Order of Distinction, Officer Class,* for his outstanding contributions to Jamaican society. He, too, is a sought-after public speaker.

Blossom O'Meally-Nelson Stokes, at the age of 84, regularly holds court in her family, social, and business circles. A pillar in Jamaican society, she served as Postmaster General, the head of two colleges, and continues to sit on the boards of for-profit and non-profit companies. Numerous national awards have been bestowed upon her. While thoroughly engaged in civic affairs, she quietly cultivated her artistic and spiritual sides. In 2010, she published a provocative book of poetry that reached deep into the darkest corners of the soul while celebrating unbound sensuality. Her journey from an itinerant preacher's wife on a poor tropical island to one of Jamaica's most prominent citizens, including the mother of two of the original Jamaican bobsledders, is testament enough for a life deserving of its own book.

Pastor Dudley Stokes Sr. died in 2010 at the age of 73. After escaping the slums of Kingston, he emerged as one of the most influential Jamaicans of his era. Notably, he rose to become one of the country's finest educators and most respected religious leaders. As the editor and manager of *The Gleaner*, he maintained the paper's feisty, critical independence despite political violence. He frequently angered politicians and avoided the cocktail circuit. Pastor Dudley was born to lead while marching to the beat of his own drum. In 2008, he was awarded one of Jamaica's highest honors, the Order of Distinction. Eulogies recalled his "Einsteinian mind," big heart, and spiritual love that inspired and changed the lives of so many.

Sandy Lightbourne joined the British Army after graduating from high school in Grand Turk. After six years of military service, he embarked on a career in banking at Barclay's Bank starting in London. Advancing quickly through the ranks, Sandy returned to the Turks & Caicos in the 1980s to open and manage the first Barclay's Bank in the islands. He always remembered how the Stokes family took him in as one of their own more than six decades ago. To this day, he remains close with all of them.

William Maloney moved from Jamaica back to his hometown of Seattle, Washington, with his wife and children in the late 1990s, following concerns about crime. He always enjoyed living in Jamaica, where he is widely respected for being the essential catalyst for Jamaican bobsledding and the early organizer that helped propel the team to the 1988 and 1992 Winter Olympics. Building on the expertise developed while living in Jamaica, Will has become one of the world's leading experts in ethanol production, now with a focus on Hawaii. He and Tal continue to stay in touch as close friends.

George Fitch died of cancer in 2016 at the age of 68 after serving four terms as the popular mayor of the small town of Warrenton in Northern Virginia. He had moved to Warrenton in 1998 because that's where his wife, Patrica, had strong roots, and she wanted to return home. Not surprisingly, George brought his energy and hustle to expand municipal services to the pleasant historical village nestled between the sprawling suburbs and bucolic countryside. While Warrenton was light-years from the exotic places in Asia and the Caribbean where George had spent most of his life, he adapted well and made it his home. Along with Will, George is widely recognized in Jamaica for his crucial role in starting Jamaica's first bobsled team from scratch and taking it to the Olympics.

Howard Siler died in Florida in 2014 at the age of 69. Although he was the first coach to teach the Jamaicans how to slide down an ice track, he never reconnected with Tal or the other Jamaican bobsledders after the 1988 Olympics. Howard is sometimes said to have been the model for the coach portrayed as Irv Blitzer in *Cool Runnings*. However, Howard displayed none of the rancorous characteristics of the fictional *Cool Runnings* coach. Howard's wife said that he was disappointed in the movie because it portrayed Jamaican athletes as "cutesy, silly," not the committed athletes he had coached.

P.C. Harris lives in Toronto, where he is actively engaged in content development for TV, film, event, and music production with Jamaican and Caribbean themes. He continues to help the Jamaica Bobsleigh Federation with their media projects and cherishes the long association that has opened many doors for him. Most recently, he has opened a luxury travel company. PC has a book in the making about how he and others used new and novel concepts to build the Jamaican bobsled team brand from Calgary through *Cool Runnings* and how it can work today.

Pat Brown stopped at a lonely gas station in Nevada in 2014 while trailering a bobsled behind his truck on his way back to New York. A skinny black man with dreadlocks and a raw Jamaican accent came up and asked Pat about the bobsled. It turned out to be **Freddie Powell**. They hugged and reminisced about the early days of the team before saying good-bye and going their separate ways. A few months later, Freddie died alone in a hotel room in Arizona. In 2020, Chris invited Pat back to be the Jamaican bobsled driver coach. Pat had always believed that driving was more important than pushing and is now in a position to impart what he has learned.

Devon Harris lives in New York City. He is the only member of the Jamaican bobsled team to turn his association into a professional career as a motivational speaker. Devon has written two books about his bobsledding experience, *Keep On Pushing: Hot Lessons from Cool Runnings*, and a children's book, *Yes I Can: The Story of the Jamaican Bobsled Team*. He also founded a philanthropic organization, *Keep On Pushing* (keeponpushing.org), which focuses on providing free breakfasts to school kids in the Kingston ghettos where he grew up and other disadvantaged communities.

John Morgan continues to be the voice of Olympic bobsledding as a commentator for NBC Sports. As he has for the past 40 years, he calls races and teams as he sees them with the same verve, passion, and plain talk that has made him a broadcasting icon. John lives in his hometown of Lake Placid, where he remains deeply involved in developing American bobsledders. He also continues to help Jamaican bobsledders train on the Mt. Van Hoevenberg Olympic Track.

Sepp Haidacher died in 2019 at the age of 78 after years of failing health. Tal flew to Austria for Sepp's funeral and said of him, "Sepp was our bobsleigh 'Godfather' and remains the spiritual center of the Jamaica Bobsleigh Federation." Every Jamaican bobsledder would likely agree.

Leo Campbell lives in Florida and works for Microsoft as the Global Business Programs Director, where he designs sales programs. Leo's leadership, discipline, and engaging manner that marked him for success early in life have not waned, as he has succeeded in every enterprise he has ever been involved with. He continues to be an informal advisor to the Jamaican Bobsleigh Federation and is widely admired in Jamaica as one of the country's bobsledding pioneers. Without his organizing skills at a critical time, the team may well have collapsed.

Trond Knaplund died in January 2023 in Norway. While coaching the Jamaican bobsled team in the early 2000s, he married one of Jamaica's talented up-and-coming drivers, Portia Morgan. They moved back to Norway, where he hoped to continue coaching her for international competition. He, too, is recognized by the Jamaican Bobsleigh Federation for stepping in when the team's future looked bleak and taking their training to the next level. Trond always loved Jamaica and the adventure of advancing the country's bobsled program.

Sam Bock continues to research and promote effective nutrition through Paragon Sciences, a company he co-founded that is based in Montreal.

Sammy Clayton died of COVID in New York in 2021 and never revealed the reason he left the team after it had qualified for the Calgary Olympics in 1988. Chris said of Sammy, "Without his sense of humor and calm spirit, I am not sure the team would have been able to hold it together in those early months."

Winston Watt retired from bobsledding after failing to qualify for the 2006 and 2010 Winter Olympics. At the age of 46, he came out of retirement to qualify for the 2014 Games in Sochi in the two-man race, placing 27 out of 30. He now lives in Evanston, Wyoming, where he imports and refurbishes classic cars, but he also stays close to the bobsled track in nearby Park City, Utah.

Wayne Thomas retired from bobsledding after the 1998 Olympics in Nagano but returned to be the coach and travel manager for the Winston Watt/Marvin Dixon team at the 2014 Olympics in Sochi. He lives in Jamaica.

Michael White and **Caswell Allen** could not be found.

THANK YOUS

The writing of a book, as with any noteworthy accomplishment, involves just about everyone the author has spent any meaningful time with over the course of a life. Let this author start the essential acknowledgements by thanking the wonderful and supportive extended Stubenberg family in Hawaii on my father's side and the Heryford family in California on my mother's side. Grandparents, uncles, aunts, and cousins. They were all there for me growing up, which is as meaningful today as it was when I was a child.

I cannot thank my mother, Jackie, enough for her guidance and unconditional love. More than anyone, she kindled a sense of adventure and encouraged me to believe that I could be anything I wanted to be. She made me write letters to relatives at an early age, which first got me thinking like a writer. Thanks also to my artist father Stanley, whose provocative, counterintuitive way of thinking always challenged established ways of doing things and encouraged me to do the same.

Thanks to my sister, Lisa, and brother, Willie, who not only stood as strong as any sister and brother could with their own unconditional love but also for their belief in me to do good things with my life. Give them credit too for not only listening but also for challenging my rambling pronouncements and sometimes setting me straight.

Thanks to my sons Mark and Matthew for their constant, unwavering support of my writing as well as all my other wild ventures. They constantly poked and prodded me with spirited banter that often escalated into uproarious debates. I ran my book's drafts by them, and they never held back where it fell short. Both make me as proud as any dad could be for all of their own unique accomplishments that continue to amaze and inspire.

Thanks to the teachers from elementary through high school who made learning fun and often fascinating. They played a critical part in shaping my talents and sensitivities, which are reflected in this book. Just as important are the many family friends who served as essential role models when it mattered. My days at University of California, Riverside and University of California, Santa Barbara, as well as at McGeorge School of Law, significantly enhanced my critical thinking, as did sparring with school friends. A big shout-out to KCSB-FM Radio at UC Santa Barbara, where I first cut my teeth on writing and broadcasting news stories.

As I entered my twenties and adulthood, I found new friends who made their mark on me in the U.S. Virgin Islands, Washington D.C., Haiti, and the Turks & Caicos Islands. All of them have been enormously encouraging.

Thank you, my lovely "partner-in-crime," Lynn Pelowski, who gives me grief, reality checks, and the heartfelt support that every writer needs to get through the day and the year.

No book is ready until proofreaders and beta readers go through it with their eagle eyes and ask, "Now, what are you trying to say here?" Thank you so much Catherine Cosgriff and Lisa Cosgriff for whipping the initial draft of the book into shape.

Thanks also to Kathy Borsuk, George Rice, Nicola Jordan, Andrea Stringos, Eney Jones, Mike Kamin, and Jim Flint for being my first beta readers and validating the readability of the book along with insightful critiques.

Kathy is also the editor and publisher of *Times of the Islands*. She always gave me free rein to write history-probing feature stories for this terrific magazine, including the article "TCI Bobsledder" that sparked the writing of this book. I am proud to be a part of a journal that brilliantly captures the people and events that define the Turks and Caicos Islands. Indeed, my Turks and Caicos Islands home overflows with an invigorating diversity of tell-it-like-it-is islanders who excite the senses and stir my passion for writing.

Now to those who played a direct and essential role in the telling of the true story of the original Jamaican bobsled team, starting with William Maloney, Leo Campbell, Blossom O'Meally-Nelson Stokes, Denise Stokes, Terrie Stokes, Pat Brown, John Morgan, Devon Harris, P.C. Harris, Todd Hays, and Ambassador Ricardo Allicock. They all generously gave their time to speak with me. This book could not have been written without them, and I deeply appreciate their essential contributions.

Thank you, Chris Stokes, for allowing me to crib from his own excellent book, *Cool Runnings and Beyond: The Story of the Jamaica Bobsleigh Team*. As a major player in Jamaican bobsledding from the Calgary Winter Olympics in 1988 right through today, Chris provided many critical facts along with nuanced perspectives that helped to drive the story forward.

Finally, the biggest thank you to Dudley Tal Stokes himself, the man who put his confidence in me to get his story right. Tal gave me hours and hours of his time and never held back on what happened. He also connected me with most of the key people who played a part in this human drama. I am eternally grateful for the opportunity to write this book about him and the original Jamaican bobsled team's incredible journey.

To anyone not mentioned, my sincere apologies. Drinks on me at Rickie's Flamingo Cafe or Omar's Beach Hut on Provo.

REFERENCES

BOOKS

Brewster, M. (2017). The night train: The story of the NASCAR-inspired bobsled that beat the world. Bo-Dyn Bobsled Project.

Steel, D. (1993). They can kill you—But they can't eat you: Lessons from the front. Pocket Books.

Stokes, C. (2002). Cool runnings and beyond: The story of the Jamaica bobsleigh team. American Book Business Press.

STATS FROM OLYMPEDIA.ORG

1988 Calgary Two-man https://www.olympedia.org/results/389

1988 Calgary Four-man https://www.olympedia.org/results/396

1992 Albertville Two-man https://www.olympedia.org/results/403

1992 Albertville Four-man https://www.olympedia.org/results/410

1994 Lillehammer Two-man https://www.olympedia.org/results/417

1994 Lillehammer Four-man https://www.olympedia.org/results/424

1998 Nagano Two-man https://www.olympedia.org/results/431

1998 Nagano Four-man https://www.olympedia.org/results/438

GENERAL

10 reasons why we love 'Shitamachi', Tokyo's traditional downtown areas! (2019, July 8). Live Japan. https://livejapan.com/en/article-a0001893/

Abrams, J. (2022, February 20). Bobsleds come down fast. New York Times. https://www.nytimes.com/2022/02/17/sports/olympics/bobsled-olympics.html

Barr, B. (n.d.). Bobsled expert explains how weather affects sliding events at the Winter Olympics. AccuWeather. https://www.accuweather.com/en/weather-news/q-and-a-bobsled-expert-explains-how-weather-affects-sliding-events-at-the-winter-olympics/352372

Bass, G. (2020, September 28). How we made 'Cool Runnings', the comedy classic about the Jamaica bobsled team. The Guardian. https://www.theguardian.com/film/2020/sep/28/how-we-made-cool-runnings-comedy-classic-jamaica-bobsled-team

Bobsled 101: Equipment. (2021, October 5). NBC Olympics. https://www.nbcolympics.com/news/bobsled-101-equipment-0

Bonk, T. (1988, February 14). Winter Olympics notes: The Jamaicans arrive a hobbin' and a bobbin'. Los Angeles Times. https://www.latimes.com/archives/la-xpm-1988-02-14-sp-42881-story.html

Bracken, C. (2020, May 12). The real story behind the '88 Jamaican Olympic bobsleigh team. ABC Triple J. https://www.abc.net.au/triplej/programs/triplej-breakfast/the-real-story-behind-the-%e2%80%9988-jamaican-olympic-bobsled-team/12238990

Bradley, P. (2022, January 26). Olympic bobsled analyst John Morgan talks about the sport and upcoming Olympic Games. Midday Magazine. https://www.wamc.org/news/2022-01-26/olympic-bobsled-analyst-john-morgan-talks-about-the-sport-and-upcoming-olympic-games

Brahhin, et al. (2016). The engineering approach to winter sports (Chapter 7). Springer. https://books.google.com/books?id=W-P6zCgAAQBAJ&pg=PA184&lpg=PA184&dq=st.%20+moritz+bobsleigh+world+cup+1990&source=bl&ots=ZbQug-coHPF&sig=ACfU3U3TAFOey%20mlXvPTeLa0TUrEvR4-0oPQ&hl=en&sa=X&ved=2ahUKEwjCtvXVs4b8AhUxjLAFH-cYuDh%20AQ6AF6BAgUEAM#v=onepage&q=st.%20%20moritz%20bobsleigh%20world%20cup%201990&f=false

Chandler, M. (2005, June 19). A party's uninvited guest. Washington Post. https://www.washingtonpost.com/archive/local/2005/06/19/a-party-primarys-uninvited-guest/839c0f45-551e-40e9-8019-00ce0941a0d8/

Crane, J. (2022, February 2). Germany's secret Olympic bobsled weapon. DW. https://www.dw.com/en/winter-olympics-germanys-secret-bob-sled-weapon/a-60631338

Eddie Eagan. (n.d.). From United States Olympic & Paralympic Museum, Hall of Fame. https://usopm.org/eddie-eagan/

Eskenazi, G. (1992, February 17). Albertville; U.S. sled is seventh as Walker is blamed. New York Times. https://www.nytimes.com/1992/02/17/sports/albertville-us-sled-is-seventh-as-walker-is-blamed.html

Fitch Family Ancestry. (n.d.). Bob's Memoirs. http://www.bobfitch.com/in_Search_of_Wisdom/Chap._I__Origins.html

George Bradley Fitch Obituary. (2015, January 7). Once Time. https://www.oncetime.com/Photos/Current/George.pdf

Gitten, I. (2018, February 16). 'Cool Runnings,' a cool break from reality. Wayland Student Press Network. https://waylandstudentpress.com/62187/articles/cool-runnings-a-cool-break-from-reality/

Harrington, R. (1993, October 1). Cool runnings. Washington Post. https://www.washingtonpost.com/wp-srv/style/longterm/movies/videos/coolrunningspgharrington_a0ab8f.htm

Harrison, A. (2017). The bobsled push start: Influence on race outcome and push athlete talent identification and monitoring. East Tennessee State University. School of Graduate Studies. https://dc.etsu.edu/cgi/viewcontent.cgi?article=4752&context=etd

Highfill, S. (2018, February 9). Cool runnings: An oral history. Entertainment. https://ew.com/article/2014/02/12/cool-runnings-oral-history/

History of IBSF. (n.d.). From IBSF. https://www.ibsf.org/en/inside-ibsf/about-ibsf

House Joint Resolution No. 773. (2015, February 6). Virginia's Legislative Information System. https://lis.virginia.gov/cgi-bin/legp604.exe?151+ful+HJ773ER

Interview with Devon Harris. (2020, February 23). Sports History Weekly. https://www.sportshistoryweekly.com/stories/jamaica-bobsled-devon-harris-winter olympics,842

Ismay, J. (2020, March 10). 'We hated what we were doing': Veterans recall firebombing Japan. New York Times. https://www.nytimes.com/2020/03/09/magazine/we-hated-what-we-were-doing-veterans recall-firebombing-japan.html

Jamaica's sporting mindset means 'competitive pressure produces outstanding talent. (2022, September 14). The Voice. https://www.voice-online.co.uk/sport/2022/09/14/jamaicas-sporting-mindset-means competitive-pressure-produces-outstanding-talent/

Japanese people contributing worldwide: Small factories aim high. The Shitamachi bobsleigh heads for the Olympics. (2016). Tomodachi. https://www.japan.go.jp/tomodachi/2016/spring2016/japanese_people_contributing_worldwide.html

Jeremy Cholm. (n.d.). Bobsled 101: Glossary, Photos, Videos & More. http://www.jeremycholm.com/more/bobsled/bobsled-101

Lauretta, T. (2018, February 14). Coach for Jamaican women's bobsled team has quit and now they may not have a sled to use. Business Insider. https://www.businessinsider.com/jamaican-womens-bobsled-team-coach-quits-2018-2

Martin, M. (2014, February 12). U.S. mayor recalls putting together the first Jamaican bobsled team. NPR. https://www.npr.org/2014/02/12/275899582/u-s-mayor-recalls-putting-together-the-first-jamaican-bobsled-team

Newhan, R. (1994, February 28). '94 Winter Lillehammer Olympics: Shimer is too hot, will isn't: Bobsled: One U.S. team disqualified, the other finishes 15th. Los Angeles Times. https://www.latimes.com/archives/la-xpm-1994-02-28-sp-28207-story.html

Notice: Press tour "challenge of small factories in the Ota Ward." (2013, August 22). Foreign Press Center Japan. https://fpcj.jp/en/assistance-en/tours_notice-en/p=4811/

Olympedia (n.d). olympedia.org

Olympics: Beer company rescues Jamaican women's bobsleigh team. (2019, December 12). AfricaNews. https://www.africanews.com/2018/02/17/olympicsbeer-company-rescues-jamaican-women-s bobsleigh-team//

"Olympics bobsleigh — Not so 'Cool Runnings': 'Destructive' coach Sandra Kiriasis quits Jamaica team." (2018, February 14). Reuters. https://www.eurosport.com/bobsleigh/pyeongchang/2018/olympics-bobsleigh-not-so-coolrunnings-destructive-coach-sandra-kiriasis-quits-jamaica-team_sto6618178/story.shtml

On this day in Jamaican history: First Jamaican men's bobsled team. (n.d.). Jamaicans.com. https://jamaicans.com/first-jamaican-mens-bobsled-team/?

Osborn, H. (2022, February 9). The perfect slide: The science of bobsledding. Smithsonian. https://ssec.si.edu/stemvisions-blog/perfect-slide-science-bobsledding

OTA TOKIO Shitamachi bobsleigh. (2015, January 30). Japan Up Close. https://japanupclose.web-japan.org/tech/20150130_1.html

Parker, D. (2021, February 8). The true origins of John Candy's 'Cool Runnings'. TheThings. https://www.thethings.com/the-true-origin-of-john-candys-cool-runnings/

Professional and Olympic Athletes: Bobsled. (n.d.). Paragon Sports. https://www.paragonsciences.com/sport/athletes/pro-olympic/bobsled/

Rhett, A. (2018, February 20). Winter Olympics 2018: The physics of blazing fast bobsled runs. Wired. https://www.wired.com/story/winter-olympics-2018-the-physics-of-blazing-fast-bobsled-runs/

Roberts, R. (1993, October 2). Jamaica's frozen assets. Washington Post. https://www.washingtonpost.com/archive/lifestyle/1993/10/02/jamaicas-frozen-assets/04c28310-76f0-491e-96c4-f823b1353887/

Rosenbush, R. (1994, February 28). Winter Olympics; The bobsled is hot, but that's bad news for U.S. team. New York Times. https://www.nytimes.com/1994/02/28/sports/winter-olympics-the-bobsled-is-hot-but-that-s-bad-news-for-us-team.html

Royal-Davis, G. (n.d.). Doctor Blossom O'Meally-Nelson, CD — Saluting 60 Jamaican women. Jamaicans.com https://jamaicans.com/doctor-blossom-omeally-nelson-cd-saluting-60-jamaican-women/

Schneider, K. (1994, March 21). Exit Laughing. People. https://people.com/archive/cover-story-exit-laughing-vol-41-no-10/

Sliding competitors see global warming trend. (2005, February 26). Baltimore Sun. https://www.baltimoresun.com/2005/02/26/sliding-competitors-see-a-global-warming-trend/

Spear, K. (2014, July 24). Howard Siler dies; Olympic bobsledder coached Jamaican team. Los Angeles Times. https://www.latimes.com/local/obituaries/la-me-howard-siler-20140725-story.html

The Editors of Encyclopedia Britannica. (1999, May 27). Bobsledding | History, rules, & Facts. Encyclopedia Britannica. https://www.britannica.com/sports/bobsledding

Trivet, B. (2022, February 17). 'Cool Runnings' cast reunites 30 years later to reflect on movie. People. https://people.com/sports/beijing-olympics-cool-runnings-cast-reunite-movie-history-jamaica bobsled/

Throwback: The Jamaican bobsleigh team and the birth of "Cool Runnings." (2018, June 7). Olympics.com. https://olympics.com/en/news/throwback-the-jamaican-bobsleigh-team-and-the-birth-of-cool-runnings

Tunno, B. (n.d.). Bobsled expert explains how weather affects sliding events at Winter Olympics. Accu-Weather. https://www.accuweather.com/en/weather-news/q-and-a-bobsled-expert-explains-how-weather-affects-sliding-events-at-the-winter-olympics/352372#:~:text=The%20tracks%20are%20largely%20covered,prepare%20and%20maintain%20the%20track%3F

USA Bobsled Skeleton. (n.d.). Jazmine Fenalator. https://www.usabs.com/profiles/jazmine-fenlator-817186

Van Cycle, K. (2018, February 14). Jamaican women's bobsled coach reportedly threatens to take sled. New York Magazine. https://www.thecut.com/2018/02/jamaican-womens-bobsled-team-is-facing-another-obstacle.html

Verschoth, A. (n.d.). Spies that slide: The East German-Swiss rivalry is redolent of Cold War fiction. Vault. https://vault.si.com/vault/1988/01/27/bobsled-spies-that-slide-the-east-german-swiss-rivalry-is-redolent-of-cold-war-fiction

Volsky, G. (1987, July 19). Jamaican drug gangs thriving in U.S. cities. New York Times. https://www.latimes.com/archives/la-xpm-1988-02-14-sp-42881-story.html

Walker, S. (1998, February 6). Testing Olympic dreams on ice and snow… Among palm trees. Christian Science Monitor. https://www.csmonitor.com/1998/0206/020698.feat.sports.1.html

Watson, B. (2022, February 12). I can't retire, I've never had a job. Press-Republican. https://www.pressrepublican.com/sports/local_sports/i-can-t-retire-i-ve-never-had-a-job/%20article_2c1f8a17-7148-5e43-b58c-48a344b1c386.html

Wikipedia contributors. (n.d.). Bobsleigh at the 1988 Winter Olympics – Four man – Wikipedia. https://en.wikipedia.org/wiki/Bobsleigh_at_the_1988_Winter_Olympics_%E2%80%93_Four_man

Wikipedia contributors. (2022, August 15). Bo-Dyn Bobsled Project. Wikipedia. https://en.wikipedia.org/wiki/Bo-Dyn_Bobsled_Project

Wikipedia contributors. (2024, January 14). Cool runnings. Wikipedia. https://en.wikipedia.org/wiki/Cool_Runnings

Wilbon, M. (1998, February 7). Winter Olympics Nagano: An opening, and maybe a beginning. Washington Post. https://www.voice-on-line.co.uk/sport/2022/09/14/jamaicas-sporting-mindset-means competitive-pressure-produces-outstanding-talent/

Willis, J. (2018, February 16). How to make an Olympic bobsledder. GQ. https://www.gq.com/story/how-athletes-get-into-bobsledding

Winter Olympics Nagano 1998: Everything you need to know about bobsled. (1997). Washington Post. https://www.washingtonpost.com/wp-srv/sports/longterm/olympics1998/sport/bobsled/articles/bobsled.htm

Woodyatt, A. (2022, February 18). 'Cool Runnings': Most people die before their legacy is revealed, but I've had to live it. CNN. https://edition.cnn.com/2022/02/18/sport/cool-runnings-tal-stokes-jamaica-winter-olympics intl-spt/index.html

Yamaguchi, J. (2018, February 19). Japanese PM Abe appears set to enact revisions to pacifist Constitution. Hankyoreh. https://english.hani.co.kr/arti/english_edition/english_editorials/832732.html

Yusuf and Nabeshima. (2006). Postindustrial East Asian cities. Chapter 2 (Tokyo): Megacity Profile. (World Bank). Stanford University Press. https://documents1.worldbank.org/curated/en/438801468024634047/pdf/372570EAP0Post101OFFICIAL0USE0ONLY1.pdf

Zillgitt, J. (n.d.). Accusations of cheating follow speed on sliding track. USA Today. https://eu.usatoday.com/story/sports/olympics/sochi/2014/02/13/accusations-of-cheating bobsled-skeleton-luge/5457947/

INDEX

ABOUT THE AUTHOR

I n 2011, Ben left his government job in Washington, D.C. and moved to the Turks and Caicos Islands. The move had been a long time coming—almost a half century since he had lived on St. Croix in the US Virgin Islands in the mid-1970s, where he taught high school English and wrote for the local newspaper. As a private pilot back then, Ben took the opportunity to visit just about every island in the West Indies and later spent months living in Martinique and Haiti. The Caribbean seeped easily into his veins.

As a feature writer for the Turks and Caicos magazine, *Times of the Islands,* he explores the region's rich and turbulent history and chronicles unfolding developments and remarkable people that are shaping the future today. Ben's connection with the Caribbean comes as no surprise. He grew up in vastly different multi-cultural environments, from Honolulu, Hawaii, where he was born, to Oslo, Norway, to Stockton, California, and learned to move easily between different peoples and landscapes—often as an outsider looking in, sometimes as an insider granted access to tell a story. *The Jamaican Bobsled Captain: Dudley "Tal" Stokes and the untold story of struggle, suffering and redemption behind* Cool Runnings is his first book. Ben can be reached through his website BenStubenberg.com

Author Ben Stubenberg / Attimi Photography